JOHN:
Living Beyond
the Ordinary

JACK W. HAYFORD
Executive Editor

THOMAS NELSON
Since 1798

NASHVILLE   DALLAS   MEXICO CITY   RIO DE JANEIRO

Published in Nashville, Tennessee. Thomas Nelson is a registered trademark of Thomas Nelson, Inc.

Thomas Nelson, Inc., titles may be purchased in bulk for educational, business, fundraising, or sales promotional use. For information, please email SpecialMarkets@ThomasNelson.com.

Unless otherwise indicated, all Scripture quotations are from the New King James Version, copyright © 1979, 1980, 1982, 1990, 2004 by Thomas Nelson, Inc.

Hayford, Jack W.

John: Living Beyond the Ordinary

ISBN 13: 978-1-4185-4122-4

Printed in the United States of America
10 11 12 13 14 — 6 5 4 3 2 1

TABLE OF CONTENTS

PREFACE
What Is Abundant Life?.. *v*

KEYS OF THE KINGDOM... *vii*

INTRODUCTION
John: Living Beyond the Ordinary.. *xi*

SESSION ONE
The God-Man... *1*

SESSION TWO
In His Image *11*

SESSION THREE
Expect a Miracle 22

SESSION FOUR
Living Water.. 32

SESSION FIVE
Know the Father... 39

SESSION SIX
An Unveiled Reality.. *48*

SESSION SEVEN
On the Defense.. *56*

SESSION EIGHT
Believing Is Seeing 63

SESSION NINE

Realities of Life 71

SESSION TEN

Servant Power 80

SESSION ELEVEN

The Divine Helper 88

SESSION TWELVE

To the Glory of God 98

What Is Abundant Life?

FOR CHRISTIANS, life is defined by and contained in the Author of life. Abundant life has little to do with circumstances and everything to do with the recognition of life's purpose. God created us for Himself. If we are to experience life beyond what the world knows, we must align ourselves with God's purpose and intent. We must give all that we have and are over to Him.

In this is abundant life: we are in Him, and He in us. As you give your total self to God, God gives His total self to you. That is the supreme message of the Bible. Inherent in God's person is true; Bible-based abundance—the real possibility of health for your total being (body, mind, emotions, relationships), of your material needs being met, of having abundant life now and through eternity.

Jesus said that He came to give life—not just ordinary existence, but life in fullness, abundance, and prosperity (John 10:10; 3 John 2). On the other hand, the Enemy (Satan) comes only to steal, kill, and destroy. The line is clearly drawn. On one side is God's goodness, life, and "plenty" of all that is necessary for life (Joel 2:26; 2 Peter 1:3), and on the other side is the Enemy of our souls, who comes to rob us of God's blessings, to oppress our bodies through disease and injury, and to destroy everything that we love and hold dear.

Your first step toward experiencing abundant life is to believe that it is God's highest desire for you. The next step is to line up your highest desire with His.

Keys of the Kingdom

KEYS CAN BE SYMBOLS of possession, of the right and ability to acquire, clarify, open, or ignite. Keys can be concepts that unleash mind-boggling possibilities. Keys clear the way to a possibility otherwise obstructed!

Jesus spoke of keys: "And I will give you the keys of the kingdom of heaven, and whatever you bind on earth will be bound in heaven, and whatever you loose on earth will be loosed in heaven" (Matthew 16:19).

While Jesus did not define the "keys" He has given, it is clear that He did confer upon His church specific tools that grant us access to a realm of spiritual "partnership" with Him. The "keys" are concepts or biblical themes, traceable throughout Scripture, that are verifiably dynamic when applied with solid faith under the lordship of Jesus Christ. The "partnership" is the essential feature of this enabling grace, allowing believers to receive Christ's promise of "kingdom keys," and to be assured of the Holy Spirit's readiness to actuate their power in the life of the believer.

Faithful students of the Word of God and some of today's most respected Christian leaders have noted some of the primary themes that undergird this spiritual partnership. A concise presentation of many of these primary themes can be found in the Kingdom Dynamics feature of the *New Spirit-Filled Life Bible.* The Spirit-Filled Life Study Guide series, an outgrowth of this Kingdom Dynamics feature, provides a treasury of more in-depth insights on these central truths. This study series offers challenges and insights designed to enable you to more readily understand and appropriate certain dynamic KINGDOM KEYS.

Each study guide has twelve to fourteen lessons, and a number of helpful features have been developed to assist you in your study, each marked by a symbol and heading for easy identification.

Kingdom Key

KINGDOM KEY identifies the foundational Scripture passage for each study session and highlights a basic concept or principle presented in the text along with cross-referenced passages.

Kingdom Life

The KINGDOM LIFE feature is designed to give practical under-standing and insight. This feature will assist you in comprehending the truths contained in Scripture and applying them to your day-to-day needs, hurts, relationships, concerns, or circumstances.

 Word Wealth

The WORD WEALTH feature provides important definitions of key terms.

 Behind the Scenes

BEHIND THE SCENES supplies information about cultural beliefs and practices, doctrinal disputes, and various types of background information that will illuminate Bible passages and teachings.

 Kingdom Extra

The optional KINGDOM EXTRA feature will guide you to Bible dictionaries, Bible encyclopedias, and other resources that will enable you to gain further insight into a given topic.

 Probing the Depths

Finally, PROBING THE DEPTHS will present any controversial issues raised by particular lessons and cite Bible passages and other sources that will assist you in arriving at your own conclusions.

Each volume of the Spirit-Filled Life Study Guide series is a com-prehensive resource presenting study and life-application questions and exercises with spaces provided for recording your answers. These study guides are designed to provide all you need to gain a good, basic understanding of the covered theme and apply biblical counsel to your life. You will need only a heart and mind open to the Holy Spirit, a prayerful attitude, a pencil and a Bible to complete the studies and apply the truths they contain. However, you may want to have a notebook handy if you plan to expand your study to include the optional KINGDOM EXTRA feature.

The Bible study method used in this series employs four basic steps:

1. *Observation.* What does the text say?
2. *Interpretation.* What is the original meaning of the text?
3. *Correlation.* What light can be shed on this text by other Scripture passages?
4. *Application.* How should my life change in response to the Holy Spirit's teaching of this text?

The New King James Version is the translation used wherever Scripture portions are cited in the Spirit-Filled Life Study Guide series. Using this translation with this series will make your study easier, but it is certainly not imperative and you will profit through use of any translation you choose.

Through Bible study, you will grow in your essential understanding of the Lord, His kingdom and your place in it; but you need more. Jesus was sent to teach us "all things" (John 14:25–26). Rely on the Holy Spirit to guide your study and your application of the Bible's truths. Bathe your study time in prayer as you use this series to learn of Him and His plan for your life. Ask the Spirit of God to illuminate the text, enlighten your mind, humble your will, and comfort your heart. And as you explore the Word of God and find the keys to unlock its riches, may the Holy Spirit fill every fiber of your being with the joy and power God longs to give all His children. Read diligently on. Stay open and submissive to Him. Learn to live your life as the Creator intended. You will not be disappointed. He promises you!

ADDITIONAL OBSERVATIONS

INTRODUCTION

John: Living Beyond the Ordinary

S EVERAL OF THE New Testament books indicate for whom they were originally written. The gospel of John does not specifically indicate its intended readers. It was written, says John, "that you may believe that Jesus is the Christ, the Son of God, and that believing you may have life in His name" (20:31). This is a book for anyone who needs Jesus or needs to deepen his or her relationship with Him. You can't get much broader than that.

The Gospel of John

Have you ever had a Proverbs 18:24 friend—a friend who "sticks closer than a brother"? This kind of friend is rare and precious. A true friend—a best friend—is one of the rarest and most valuable treasures in life.

John had such a friend. His name was Jesus. John and Jesus knew each other as best friends do, but they both knew that, in spite of all they had in common, there were two things they didn't share. These two things made Jesus absolutely unique, superior to every human being, living or dead. *He was God in the flesh and completely without sin.* Nothing in John's experience could have prepared him for a close relationship with such a man. The ecstasy of it all was indescribable.

Along with the ecstasy came a soul-wrenching agony. Jesus knew He was going to die, and John knew it too. He also knew that Jesus would suffer a great deal before His death, and that hurt him deeply. John experienced the loss of his best friend—he even watched Him die.

But John also saw Jesus as the victor over death, and he dedicated the rest of his days to telling others about his best friend so they could become His friends too. That's what John's gospel is all about. It is an intimate, realistic yet mind-stretching portrayal of the Man who shook the world—John's best friend, the Son of God, the Son of man.

As you begin this study, don't forget that this gospel is the product of love: John's love for Jesus, Jesus' love for you and me, and the Father's love for His Son and the world. In such a love letter, we'll find plenty that will apply to our lives, our relationships, our values, our joys, and our pains.

The Author

This fourth gospel does not specifically identify its author, but two sources of evidence point to John.

The first source is *internal*—what the text of the gospel reveals about its author. A figure referred to as "the disciple whom Jesus loved" (John 21:20) appears often throughout the gospel. And while most of the other twelve disciples of Jesus are named, this one is not; one of the unnamed disciples is John. So by the process of elimination, the internal evidence leads to the conclusion that "the disciple whom Jesus loved" is John.

The second source of evidence is *external*—what church tradition claims about the gospel's authorship. And this tradition consistently presents John, one of the sons of Zebedee, as the author of the fourth gospel. One of these historical sources, Irenaeus, who was the bishop of Lyons in the latter half of the second century and an associate of Polycarp who had known John, heard Polycarp testify that the Lord's disciple John published the gospel of John while he was living in Ephesus.

So the evidence is quite strong that John, the beloved disciple of the Lord, wrote the gospel that bears his name. (By the way, he also wrote 1, 2, and 3 John, and the book of Revelation.)

Read Matthew 4:19–21; 17:1; 27:56; Mark 1:19; 3:17; 9:2; Luke 5:10; 9:54; John 1:35–42; 2:2; 13:23; 19:26–27; Acts 3:1–11; 4:5–21; 8:14–25; Galatians 2:9; 1 John 1:1–4; Revelation 1:9.

Questions:

What can you learn about John from these passages?

What characteristics do you share with him?

✎_____

_____

_____

What characteristics do you wish you shared with him?

✎_____

_____

_____

The Message

If you have ever read the Synoptic Gospels—Matthew, Mark, and Luke—you know that they have a lot of similar content, and they basically present the same chronology of Jesus' life and ministry, death, and resurrection. The gospel of John is much different. Its arrangement is more topical than chronological. And when a chronology presents itself, it's wrapped around the Jewish religious calendar, showing Jesus at many of the major religious festivals generating controversy over who He claims to be and what He does.

Jesus squarely faced the evil and polluted practices of the church in His day. He did not hesitate to confront ungodly situations or attitudes. His actions make it clear that He was willing to move into a situation and stir things up—not for controversy's sake, but for the stirring of interest and for the spread of God's kingdom.

Read John 2:13–25; 5:1–18; 6:4–15; 7:2–52; 10:22–39; 11:55—12:43; 13:1–5; 18:1—19:42.

Questions:

Note what religious celebration Jesus was attending and what He did in each of these passages.

✎_____

_____

_____

When was the last time the expression of your faith generated some holy commotion?

✎ _____

_____

Getting Started

With this background information in mind, it's time to read through the entire gospel and get a closer look at John's portrait of Jesus. Over the next week, read three chapters daily and develop your own brief paragraph summaries for each day's coverage. A half hour per day will allow this fruitful overview and set you in good stead for the following seasons of study.

Questions:

In your overview of John, what made a deep impression on you?

✎ _____

_____

Why do you think these things stuck out to you?

✎ _____

_____

It's not unusual to hear people complain about how hard it is to be a Christian in their community. Do you do that? What have you gleaned so far in this study that should perhaps work to change your attitude and perspective?

✎ _____

_____

_____

How about it? Are you willing to be changed?

✎ _____

_____

_____

SESSION ONE

The God-Man

John 1:1–18

Colossians 1:15–17 He is the image of the invisible God, the firstborn over all creation. For by Him all things were created that are in heaven and that are on earth, visible and invisible, whether thrones or dominions or principalities or powers. All things were created through Him and for Him. And He is before all things, and in Him all things consist.

Christianity is adamant about the central role of Jesus Christ because Jesus Christ is God in the flesh. This man, born in Bethlehem and raised in Nazareth by Mary and Joseph, is also fully God. While being cradled in Mary's arms as a baby, He was sustaining the entire universe in its existence. While feeding at Mary's breasts, He was providing nourishing rains all over the earth. While learning the trade of carpentry at Joseph's side, He was being worshipped and adored by angels. This man who ate, grew tired, became frustrated, voiced anger, perspired, suffered, cried, was misunderstood and rejected—this man was also deity who was in need of nothing, in control of everything, all-powerful, all-knowing, all-loving, perfect in every way. He is the God-man. Everything that belongs to deity, He has; everything that belongs to humanity, except for sin, He has. He is fully God yet fully man. Only Christianity affirms this truth about Jesus. So central is it that if Christianity is wrong about Jesus, then Christianity is false. Christianity is Christ. Without Him Christianity has nothing unique to say, nothing unique to give, no hope to offer, no forgiveness to promise, no salvation that can be secured, no Son, no Spirit, no Father, no nothing.

John, the human author of the fourth gospel, knows this fact very well. So in his gospel's prologue, which is made up of the first eighteen verses, he sets out the basic facts about Jesus—who He is, what He is, why He came to earth, and why we should listen to Him and not turn away. The facts presented are startling, revolutionary, heart stirring. But more than that, they are life-giving for those who have ears to hear and the will to obey.

Read Philippians 2:6–11.

Questions:

What does it mean to you personally that Jesus is fully God and fully man?

_____

_____

How should this affect your relationship with Him?

_____

_____

Parallels to Ponder

Correlation is one of the most illuminating steps of Bible study. When you use correlation, you compare passages in one part of the Bible to similar passages in another part. This process ends up throwing light on both sets of passages, so you walk away with a better understanding of the meaning of the texts.

When you read John 1:1, "In the beginning was the Word," you may have noticed that it begins like Genesis 1:1: "In the beginning God created the heavens and the earth." As you read a little further into John 1, you may have also noticed that it talks about the Word's involvement in creation, which also brings to mind the creation account of Genesis 1.

Read Genesis 1:1–24.

Questions:

What parallels can you find between John 1:1–18 and Genesis 1:1–24?

_____

_____

Why do you think John was so careful to allude to the beginning of Genesis in content and structure?

✎ _____

_____

What do you see as John's main point in his prologue? (Read John 20:31.)

✎ _____

_____

Probing the Depths

Let's take a closer look at the wording of John's beautiful prologue.

In the beginning (1:1–2): This phrase refers to the start of creation, harking back to Genesis 1:1.

Was (1:1): Indicates that the Word predates the start of creation. In other words, the Word was in existence prior to even the first act of bringing the universe into being.

With (1:1): Toward God, face-to-face with God, in company with God. The idea is that the Word was in eternal fellowship with the rest of the Godhead—God the Father and God the Holy Spirit.

God (1:1–2): In the first and third occurrences of this word, *God* refers to the Father and the Holy Spirit (the first and third members of the Godhead). The second use of the term means "deity"; it indicates the indivisible divine nature that the Word shares with the Father and the Holy Spirit.

Word (1:1): The English translation of the Greek term *logos*. To the first-century Jewish mind, *logos* meant the spoken word, with the emphasis on the meaning, not the sound, of the word, so it would imply a personal being involved in communication. Because of the similarity between John 1:1 and Genesis 1:1, Jewish readers would have connected the *Word* in John with the creative activity of God in Genesis 1, where He spoke and things came into being (Genesis 1:3). So for them, *logos* would designate the personal creative power and activity of God. It is the Word in action.

For Greek readers *logos* meant reason, rational thought, and discourse; the principle of reason or order in the world that gives the world its form and makes up the soul of man. We get our word *logic* from *logos*.

Together, these meanings tell us that the Word is the personal, rational source of power and action in creation. The apostle John undoubtedly chose this word so it would appeal to Jews and Greeks, conveying truths both groups would associate with the Word.

Nothing (1:3): Not even one thing was made apart from the creative work of the Word.

Read 1 John 5:7; Revelation 19:11–13.

Questions:

Why do you think these verses refer to Jesus as "the Word"?

_____

_____

_____

How can the Word be the same as God, yet different?

_____

_____

_____

Behind the Scenes

One of the most difficult doctrines in Christianity is the Trinity. When John talks about the sameness between the Word and God, yet also indicates difference, he raises a problem that Christians have always accepted but that took a few hundred years to resolve. The Bible makes it very clear that there is only one God. But the Bible also clearly states that the Father is God, Jesus Christ is God, and the Holy Spirit is God.

The fourth-century church formally articulated the relationship between the Father, the Son, and the Holy Spirit as three uncreated, eternal, coequal persons coexisting in or sharing the same indivisible divine nature. Therefore, each person is fully God, possessing exactly the same divine attributes because each shares exactly the same nature, yet each person is eternally distinct. In short, there is only one God, but this God is three distinct persons eternally coexisting in one divine nature.

If you find this difficult to understand, you're not alone! Shouldn't the God of all the universe be slightly beyond description? As you study the teachings of the Bible regarding the Trinity, know that throughout the centuries the church has upheld this understanding of God as a faithful description of what the Bible teaches. Truly great minds are consistently willing to acknowledge their finite grasp and to leave room for the possibility that the transcendent greatness of God might exceed their full grasp. Yet in the personal nature of His love, God has chosen to reveal Himself to us.

Read Deuteronomy 6:4; Isaiah 44:6–8; 45:5–6, 18, 21–22; 1 Corinthians 8:4–6; 1 Timothy 2:5 (one God). Read John 6:27; Romans 1:7; Galatians 1:1 (the Father). Read John 1:1–3, 14; Colossians 2:9; Titus 2:13; Hebrews 1:2–3; 1 John 5:20 (the Son). Read Acts 5:3–4; 28:25–27; 2 Corinthians 3:16–17; Hebrews 10:15–16 (the Holy Spirit). Read Matthew 28:18–19; 1 Corinthians 1:3; 2 Corinthians 13:14; Ephesians 4:4–6 (divine attributes).

Questions:

What is your personal relationship with each person of the Trinity?

_____

_____

_____

In what ways has God revealed Himself to you?

_____

_____

_____

How might you come to know Him (Father, Son, and Holy Spirit) to a greater degree?

_____

_____

_____

Kingdom Life—*The Word Made Flesh*

"And the Word became flesh and dwelt among us" (John 1:14). Because God is so difficult to comprehend, Jesus became a man revealing the essence of the Father and proclaiming truth concerning God (John 1:14, 18). The gospel accounts of the ministry of Christ make it easier for us to understand what God is like. We see God revealed in the person of Jesus through a love that is boundless, a power that is without limit, and a compassion that is constant and complete.

Jesus is completely God and also completely man. While He walked sinlessly when clothed in flesh, He faced every temptation we could ever face. There is no struggle against sin with which our Savior is unfamiliar.

Read Luke 10:22; Hebrews 2:18; 4:15; 1 Corinthians 10:13.

Questions:

What are the greatest temptations in your life?

_____

_____

How can you see that Jesus might have experienced these?

_____

_____

_____

What weapons did Jesus use to overcome temptation? (See Matthew 4:1–11.)

_____

_____

Kingdom Life—*The Light of Men*

John refers to Jesus as "Light" throughout the opening verses of his gospel. John uses this name for Jesus in an attempt to describe and clarify the essence and mission of the incarnate Word. In order to more fully grasp John's intent, it is important to consider the qualities that light possesses.

Read John 1:7–8; 2 Corinthians 4:3–6; Ephesians 5:8–10; Matthew 5:14–16.

Questions:

List the qualities of light. How does each give insight into the essence and mission of Jesus?

_____

_____

_____

What insight does this give as to your own mission in the kingdom?

_____

_____

_____

What are the qualities of darkness?

_____

_____

_____

To what do you believe the uncomprehending darkness in John 1:5 refers?

_____

_____

_____

Word Wealth—*Comprehend*

Comprehend: Greek *katalambano* (kat-al-am-ban'-o); Strong's *#2638*: This word has three separate meanings: (1) To seize, lay hold of, overcome. As such John 1:5 could read, "The darkness does not gain control of it." (2) To perceive, attain, lay hold of with the mind: to apprehend with mental or moral effort. With this meaning the verse could be translated, "The darkness is unreceptive and does not understand it." (3) To quench, extinguish, snuff out the light by stifling it." With this meaning the thought conveyed in the verse is: "The darkness will never be able to eliminate it." Light and darkness essentially are antagonistic. The Christian's joy is in knowing that light is not only greater than darkness, but will also outlast the darkness.

Kingdom Life—*Know Him*

John's gospel records various testimonies concerning Christ, showing that faith in Him is based upon evidence. The witness of John the Baptist—as well as Jesus' life, death, and resurrection—makes the world's rejection of Jesus inexcusable. By His coming Jesus became the true light to those who believe, but He is also the light that, in a general sense, enlightens the human conscience and thereby makes all mankind responsible before God.

The word translated as "know" in verse 10 literally means to "recognize truth by personal experience." Even so, the new birth does not come by physical descent, human effort, or human volition but by the power of God.

Read John 6:44, 65; Ephesians 2:8; Philippians 2:12–13.

Questions:

With these verses in mind, what is required of us for our salvation?

_____

_____

_____

What do you suppose it means to "work out your own salvation with fear and trembling" (Philippians 2:12)?

_____

_____

_____

Probing the Depths

Before the Word came, God had revealed Himself in the world in a variety of ways throughout history (Hebrews 1:1). A quick review of the Old Testament will confirm that God revealed Himself at every turn: the burning bush, the pillar of fire, through the tabernacle, and through the system of sacrifice. These are only a few of the acts of God designed to reveal His nature and character to humankind.

But John says that "no one has seen God at any time" (1:18). Given all the ways God manifested Himself in the Old Testament, John must have been speaking of a "knowing" that transcends the five senses.

Read Proverbs 8:17; Jeremiah 29:13–14.

Questions:

What made the revelation of God in the Word unique (John 1:14, 17–18)?

_____

_____

_____

How can you then explain John's statement that no one has ever seen the Father?

_____

_____

_____

A Glorious Truth

In introducing the incarnation, John presents us with another very difficult teaching: Jesus was completely man and completely God. The Word, the Son of God, took upon Himself a fully human nature (body, soul, and spirit), one just like ours yet untainted by sin, so He now had two distinct natures: one fully human and another fully divine. And this God-man made His dwelling place among men. God no longer dwelt in a tabernacle made by human hands but in His incarnate Son.

The revelation of God that came through the prophet Moses came through the law. Although God's grace and truth were seen in the law, they have been manifested in Jesus Christ in such fullness that there is hardly any comparison between the two revelations. We have received "grace for grace" (John 1:16), one wave of grace being constantly replaced by another. Grace heaped upon grace, grace overflowing.

Record Your Thoughts

The gospel of John introduces some very difficult doctrines, some we may never fully understand. Yet, as John daily walked with Jesus and pursued an intimate knowledge of the Holy One, so should we. And one day, we shall know even as we are known.

Questions:

What has most impacted you through your study of this session?

_____

_____

_____

Reread John 1:1–11. What new revelations have you found?

_____

_____

_____

What questions has this session answered for you?

_____

_____

_____

What other questions has it posed?

_____

_____

_____

To gain a greater understanding of the Trinity and the incarnation, you may wish to locate trusted literature on the subject. You can't plumb the depths of these doctrines without receiving personal benefits, so go ahead—dive in. It will be well worth your time and effort.

SESSION TWO

In His Image
John 1:19—2:25

 Kingdom Key—We Are Formed for a Purpose

Jeremiah 29:11 I know the thoughts that I think toward you, says the LORD, thoughts of peace and not of evil, to give you a future and a hope.

We all have a basic need to have our own identities, to be our own persons. While we want to fit in and belong, we don't want to become absorbed by others. We want to stand out from the crowd, even lead the crowd. We want to carve out and retain our own identities.

Why is this drive so strong? The reason is simple: God designed us this way. "I want to be me" is not the refrain of egotism but of individuals created in God's image who long to discover who they are and fulfill their life's purpose. People don't always understand this about themselves, but that doesn't discount the fact that God has designed them to pursue self-discovery and self-fulfillment.

In this passage we learn about a man who was sure about who he was and his calling and four other people who began to discover what God had created them to do with their lives. Regardless of how far you have come in understanding yourself and your life purpose, this portion of John can help you move even closer to grasping these basic, God-ordained goals.

Read Psalm 139:15–16; Ephesians 2:10; Romans 8:28–30.

Questions:

Can you look to the past and know God's purpose for you during those times?

_____

_____

Can you look toward the future and know God's purpose for you in days to come?

✎ _____

_____

_____

What is God's purpose for you today?

✎ _____

_____

_____

Kingdom Life—*Know Your Purpose*

The story of "the voice of one crying in the wilderness" (Isaiah 40:3; John 1:23) is a familiar one to most. John the Baptist had been prophesied centuries before his birth. In this passage John answers questions about his identity directed to him by the priests and Levites. His answer proves his absolute certainty of his own destiny. He knew exactly who he was and what his purpose in God's kingdom would be. And he embraced this calling with his entire being.

We can stand as firmly as John the Baptist and walk with as much assurance when we know our calling and purpose. Although we may not have ancient prophecies revealing God's plan for our lives, we can know our purpose just as surely as John. Jesus did not leave us alone, wondering and wandering. He sent us His Spirit to guide and direct us. We need only listen to His word in our hearts. He will call forth the deep things within us and set us on a path to our kingdom destiny.

Read John 16:13; Ephesians 2:10.

Questions:

Why does knowing God's plan for our lives produce a greater degree of commitment?

✎ _____

_____

_____

What are the consequences of being unaware of God's call on your life?

✎_____

_____

_____

Where do you believe the Lord is guiding you in this regard?

✎_____

_____

_____

Behind the Scenes

The priests were the theological authorities. Descendants of Aaron, the priests had the primary job of ministering at the altar in the temple (Exodus 28:1).

The Levites were descendants of Levi, and they had been appointed to assist the priests with the temple rituals and service (Numbers 8:19, 26).

Unlike the priests and Levites, whose beginnings were instituted by God in the Old Testament law, the Pharisees came on the scene at the end of the second century B.C. The Pharisees believed that the written and oral traditions of the rabbis were as authoritative as the written law of Moses. The rabbis' traditions were basically theological and practical commentaries on the Mosaic law, and they were developed to ensure that the law's principles would remain applicable to the changes of Jewish society. By preserving and following these traditions, the Pharisees were trying to safeguard the law from being dismissed as irrelevant or obsolete.

The name *Pharisees* means "separated ones," and that's how the members of this group were best known. In their religious devotion they separated themselves from everything that might convey or lead to ethical or ceremonial impurity. According to the Jewish historian Josephus, himself a follower of their principles, the Pharisees had the reputation of following the law to the letter. They were an influential minority among the Jewish religious leaders during the days of Jesus.

Kingdom Life—*Possess Your Own Territory*

John knew exactly what his ministry was and made sure others knew it too. He was to pave the way for the expected Deliverer, who would eventually die at the hands of the Romans under the charge of insurrection (John 19:12–19).

According to Malachi 4:5, the prophet Elijah was to come before the Messiah. Even though John looked and sounded like the expected Elijah and had a ministry similar to his (Luke 1:13–17, 76–79), John denied the imposed identification. He came in Elijah's power and office, but he was not the resurrected prophet.

Many Jews also expected a prophet like Moses to arise before the Messiah's arrival (Deuteronomy 18:15–19). They hoped this prophet would deliver them from their enemies in a new exodus, and they expected him to be a separate individual from the Messiah. They were wrong on both counts. Jesus was the fulfillment of this Old Testament expectation, and He was not the Jews' political deliverer.

John knew who he was: the voice in the wilderness, the herald of the Lord, the way-preparer for the Messiah, the witness-bearer of the true Light. Because his self-identity and calling were sure in his mind, he could make them clear to others and be effective in his mission.

How often do we see folks in the kingdom determined to fulfill an office or task when they are obviously not equipped to do so? More problems have been created by these well-meaning ones than can be numbered.

Questions:

Can you think of instances where ill-equipped, would-be ministers have created or intensified problems?

_____

_____

How can you guard against this in your own life?

_____

_____

The Lamb of God

In the Old Testament lambs are connected to a number of sacrifices: the Passover (Exodus 12:3–14); the daily temple sacrifice (Exodus 29:38–41); the burnt offering (Leviticus 1:10); the peace offering (Leviticus 3:7); the sin offering (Leviticus 4:32); the purification of a leper (Leviticus 14:13); the Feast of Trumpets, the Feast of Tabernacles, and the Day of Atonement (Numbers 29:1–40). All of these sacrifices are likely implied by the title "the Lamb of God" (John 1:29). But because so much of the fourth gospel is developed around the Passover Feast, the Passover sacrifice may be the primary one in view. The primary teaching contained in the Passover was that deliverance was purchased through the shedding of innocent blood. The guilty were saved by the sacrifice of the innocent. John's words in verse 29 would have caused the listening Jews to link his remark to the lamb sacrificed at Passover. They rightly concluded that John was claiming that Jesus was God's sacrificial Lamb, who by shedding His blood would remove the world's sins (1 Corinthians 5:7; Revelation 5:6–14).

Locate other passages where Jesus is referred to as the "Lamb."

Question:

Jesus also calls Himself the Shepherd of His people. Why do you think He wants us to know Him as both Shepherd and Lamb?

 Word Wealth—*Witness*

Witness: Greek *martus* (mar'-toos); Strong's *#3144*: One who testifies to the truth he has experienced, a witness, one who has knowledge of a fact and can give information concerning it.

Also translated "testimony," the term *martus*, or "witness," occurs nearly fifty times in John's gospel. The apostle John uses it in two ways: (1) to indicate what is legally acceptable testimony to prove the truth of something (John 8:17), and (2) to show that a commitment has been made to that truth. The truth witnessed to is Jesus, and in the fourth gospel the witnesses are John the Baptist (1:6–7, 34); a variety of other human beings, including the disciples (15:27) and the crowds who saw Jesus' incredible deeds (12:17); Jesus' own works (5:36; 10:25); Scripture (5:39); the Father (5:31–32, 37); the Holy Spirit (15:26); and, of course, Jesus Himself (8:14, 18). The point is that there are more than enough witnesses to establish the truth about Jesus' identity and mission.

Baptism

What were the differences between John's baptism and Jesus' (1:33)? Look up the passages listed below, then note in the appropriate column what they say about Jesus' baptism and John's.

SCRIPTURES	JESUS' BAPTISM	JOHN'S BAPTISM
Ezekiel 36:25–27		
Joel 2:28–30		
Matthew 3:11–12		
Mark 1:4–5		
Luke 24:49		
John 7:38–39		
Acts 2:5–41		
Acts 19:1–6		
1 Corinthians 12:13		

Read Matthew 28:18–20; Acts 1:5–8.

Questions:

Have you been baptized in water as Jesus commanded? Tell what happened.

✎ _____

_____

Have you been baptized in the Holy Spirit as Jesus promised? Tell what happened.

✎ _____

_____

Kingdom Extra

Jesus' question to the two disciples who followed Him after John the Baptist proclaimed Him the "Son of God" (John 1:34) seems a bit odd: "What do you seek?" (v. 38). Jesus stressed the *what* rather than the *who* of the situation. Could it be that Jesus questioned their motivation so they would truly seek their hearts before following Him?

When asked where He was staying, Jesus' answer to them was just as provocative as His question: "Come and see" (v. 39). Jesus knew that their fledgling faith needed proof; His first disciples would need to hear and experience much before they were able to live out the call on their lives.

Jesus' answer to these two disciples is just as relevant now as it was then. Until we have entered into an intimate fellowship with our Lord, we cannot fulfill our kingdom destiny. A life of ultimate purpose and fulfillment awaits the one who will "come and see."

Read Psalm 34:8; Matthew 6:33.

Questions:

Consider Jesus' words "Come and see." What further reason can you find for His use of this brief answer?

✎ _____

_____

How might living by these words change your perception of yourself and the world around you?

_____

_____

How might these words be used to minister truth to others?

_____

_____

Word Wealth—*Messiah*

Messiah: Hebrew *mashiach* (maw-shee'-akh); Strong's #4899: Anointed one, messiah. Found thirty-nine times in the Old Testament, *mashiach* is derived from the verb *mashach,* meaning to anoint or the act of consecrating an individual by applying holy anointing oil. The kings and priests of Israel were anointed. But the word *mashiach* is particularly used for David's anointed heir, the king of Israel and ruler of all nations. (See Psalms 2:2; 28:8; Daniel 9:25–26.) When the earliest followers of Jesus spoke of Him, they called Him Jesus the Messiah, or in Hebrew *Yeshua ha-Mashiach.* "Messiah" or "Anointed One" is *Christos* in Greek and is the origin of the English word *Christ.* Whenever the Lord is called "Jesus Christ," He is being called "Jesus the Messiah."

Probing the Depths

When Simon met Jesus, Jesus changed Simon's name (John 1:42). This name has been understood differently by different denominations.

Most Protestant denominations believe that the rock is not Peter as an individual, but that Jesus may have meant that He Himself is the Rock (*petra,* meaning foundation rock or boulder) upon which the church is built and that the church is built out of those stones (*petros,* meaning fragment of the *petra*) that partake of the nature of the *petra* by their confession of faith in Jesus, the Rock (*petra*). Peter, therefore, is the first of many building stones in the church.

However, some denominations believe that Jesus proclaimed in these words that Peter was to be the foundation rock upon which Jesus would build His church. As such, upon Jesus' death and resurrection, Peter became the leader of the new Christian church.

Though hotly debated for centuries, this is not a matter of eternal consequence and should not create a schism in the body of Christ. We do not preach the gospel of Peter or John or any other man—only the gospel of Jesus Christ. We all agree that He is the Petra—the Rock on which we stand.

Read Matthew 16:18; Luke 22:31–32; John 21:15–19.

Questions:

What is your understanding of these verses?

_____

_____

In what ways do you experience Jesus as the Rock in your own life?

_____

_____

What differences might you experience in the midst of trial if you recognized Him as your Rock to a greater degree?

_____

_____

Must you feel like you are standing on the Rock in order for this to be so?

_____

_____

Nathanael

While on the surface Nathanael's question "Can anything good come out of Nazareth?" (John 1:46) may seem insulting, it was not meant to be so. Nathanael knew that Nazareth was an obscure location and was not the prophesied birthplace of the Messiah. When Philip proclaimed Jesus as the fulfillment of the Old Testament prophecies of a coming Messiah, Nathanael voiced his doubt to Philip's assertion.

However, Jesus' supernatural insight into Nathanael's character convinced him that Jesus was indeed the Son of God, the King of Israel. Even through the facade of Nathanael's skepticism, Jesus discerned his transparency of spirit. Where we may have seen doubt, Jesus saw hope. Where we may have seen faithlessness, Jesus saw fertile ground. Our eyes are deceptive. It is only through Jesus that we can clearly see.

Read Matthew 7:1–5; Luke 6:37.

Question:

Jesus' closing words to Nathanael (John 1:51) are reminiscent of Jacob's dream in Genesis 28:10–15. Why would Jesus allude to this event? What point was He making to Nathanael?

Kingdom Life—*Blessed Assurance*

Jesus often used the words "most assuredly." This is a phrase of solemn affirmation meant to express certainty that what is said is trustworthy and will be fulfilled.

Jesus could not have won the support of so many people so quickly unless He was self-assured about His identity as the Father's Son and His mission as the Father's chosen Savior. Jesus knew what He was all about; His actions and the responses He received revealed that. We saw the same thing with John the Baptist. You don't have to be God's Son to have that kind of assurance, but when you know you're rightly related to Him, following Him His way, that kind of assurance will come.

So keep looking to Him, as John and the other disciples did. The rest will take care of itself.

Record Your Thoughts

We have discussed in this session the importance of knowing who we are and to what we are called. Yet many of us struggle to ascertain exactly what the Lord's call on our lives may be. It is important we recognize that after Jesus says, "Come and see," He also tells His followers to go and tell (Matthew 28:19). This is our overriding purpose and our great honor. It is not of importance that you discover a title or position for which the Lord has fashioned you, but it is joy beyond telling to walk moment by moment in the center of His will. It is doubtful the apostles realized as they lived their daily lives that their words and actions would be a guiding light to many generations to come. They simply lived their faith and followed the Lord's leading throughout their days. This is the model we would do well to follow. We will find our destinies fulfilled only when we look to the One who created us, and then only as we learn to say with Paul, "It is no longer I who live, but Christ lives in me" (Galatians 2:20).

Questions:

Do you seek the Lord's leading throughout your daily life?

_____

_____

_____

How might doing so affect your attitude and actions?

_____

_____

_____

Is there a position or title to which you aspire?

_____

_____

_____

Is this the leading of the Lord or your own desire? Why do you believe this is so?

_____

_____

_____

SESSION THREE

Expect a Miracle

John 3:1–36

Philippians 3:12–14 Not that I have already attained, or am already perfected; but I press on, that I may lay hold of that for which Christ Jesus has also laid hold of me. Brethren, I do not count myself to have apprehended; but one thing I do, forgetting those things which are behind and reaching forward to those things which are ahead, I press toward the goal for the prize of the upward call of God in Christ Jesus.

Expectations. We all have them, and we order our lives around them. They motivate us, change us, challenge us, and sometimes even disturb us. They can lift us up or let us down, crown us or trash us. Their fulfillment can elude us for years, even a lifetime. And yet at times they come to fruition faster than we could have ever hoped or feared. Often the way in which they finally become realities knocks us off our feet, like being tripped in the dark. Sometimes we jump back up with joy; sometimes we never stand as tall again; for some of us, the pain can be so great that we never even get up.

Among first-century Jewish people, the expectations for the Messiah who was to come were at an all-time high. The Jews were being ruled by Gentiles—Romans—and, understandably, they hated it. They longed to be out from under the heavy hand of the Roman Empire and so kept watch for a military Messiah, a political Deliverer (Psalm 2; Isaiah 11—12; Daniel 7).

Although some people looked to Jesus as their mighty Warrior-King, He would have none of it (John 6:14–15). His mission and ways were different, which confused and disillusioned many of His Jewish contemporaries, even some of His disciples. Others felt threatened and tried to kill Him, and one of His own would betray Him. Some, however, would see in Him their salvation, and they would believe in Him and find it. All would view Him with expectations, and some would have their expectations fulfilled, while others would see them fall away.

Let's see how He measures up to your expectations.

Signs of Revelation

Excluding the resurrection and the miraculous catch of fish recorded in John 21:4–11, John records seven signs (miracles), each designed to reveal something about the person of Christ, to authenticate His message, and to point to the future kingdom of the Messiah (Isaiah 35:5–6). The first of these signs is found in John 2, and we'll deal with it in more detail in just a bit. For now, read through the passages below, then jot down the sign and what it unveils about Jesus, His message, and/or His kingdom. This helps us see how signs are used by the Lord in His ministry, not as entertainment or gimmicks but as demonstrations of deity to verify His supernatural presence and power.

The Seven Signs

SCRIPTURE	SIGN	SIGNIFICANCE
2:1–11	Turning water-wine	Reveal Glory
4:46–54	Healing Royal Son	Reveal
5:1–9	Heals paralytic man	Compassion
6:1–14	Fed the Five thousand	met their needs
6:16–21	Jesus walked on water	dominion over
9:1–12	Jesus heals blindman	Work of creation God to display
11:1–46	(Raised Lazarus) showed who Jesus was.	

Kingdom Life—*To Everything a Season*

The scene of the first sign takes place "in Cana of Galilee" (John 2:1), which was about seventy-five miles from Bethany, the place Jesus had been gathering His disciples (1:28), and about eight miles from His hometown of Nazareth. The occasion was a Jewish wedding feast that lasted anywhere from one to seven days, depending on the new husband's resources. It was a time of tremendous joy and celebration, and Jesus, His disciples, and His mother had all been invited (2:1–2).

Knowing who her son was, Mary asked Him to perform a miracle. Jesus' response, "My hour has not yet come" (2:4), carried two meanings: (1) "It is not yet time for Me to act," which would refer to Jesus' looking for the appropriate moment to replenish the wine supply; and (2) "It is not yet time for Me to be glorified," which, while happening to a degree after the miracle occurs, still doesn't find its ultimate fulfillment until Jesus' crucifixion and resurrection.

Jesus' example to us here is that "to everything there is a season, a time for every purpose under heaven" (Ecclesiastes 3:1). It seems to be in our very nature to face life with impatience, to presume too much, or push too hard. Jesus, however, moved in perfect synchronization with the Father.

Read John 7:6–8; 8:20; 12:23–33; 13:1; 16:32; 17:1.

Questions:

Can you recall a time when you rushed a relationship or circumstance without considering God's timing and listening closely for His guidance? What was the result?

_____

_____

How can you move in God's timing rather than your own?

_____

_____

Probing the Depths

After leaving Cana and spending some time in Capernaum with His mother, brothers, and disciples, Jesus traveled to Jerusalem for the Passover (John 2:12–13). This passage raises a point of debate in the Christian church—whether Jesus had younger siblings.

The references to brothers and sisters in relationship to Jesus Christ (Mark 6:3; John 7:2–10) have been given three interpretations. Traditional Catholic commentators, who propose the doctrine of the perpetual virginity of Mary, believe that these references indicate either Jesus' cousins or Joseph's children by a previous marriage. Protestant commentators generally accept the view that these references describe the younger children born to Mary and Joseph. Perhaps the best attitude to take on this matter is historian Paul Maier's: although theologians may debate the issue, most of Christianity can go along quite well with either interpretation. The New Testament tends to generalize regarding points that are not central to faith.

Behind the Scenes

The Passover has its roots in the Old Testament. The celebration is connected with one of the most important events in Israel's history—the exodus of the Hebrews from slavery in Egypt. Read about the establishing of the Passover in Exodus 12. If you can, you may want to consult a Bible dictionary or encyclopedia as well.

Associated with the Passover was the annual temple offering (Exodus 30:13–16), both of which took place in Jerusalem. Pilgrims traveling to Jerusalem for these religious events had to exchange their Roman money for the Jewish half-shekel. Because Jews were required by law to spend a tenth of their income in Jerusalem (Deuteronomy 14:23–27), citizens of Jerusalem quite willingly filled the visitors' needs. This included selling to worshippers—at a healthy profit, of course—the animals they would need for their sacrifices (John 2:14).

Kingdom Life—*Seek the Giver, Not the Gift*

After cleansing the temple of these greed-poisoned peddlers, Jesus stayed in Jerusalem to celebrate the Passover Feast. He also performed a number of miraculous signs that led many more people to believe "in His name" (John 2:23). But verses 24 and 25 indicate that Jesus didn't respond to their faith profession as He had to His disciples'. These people responded to the supernatural miracles, not to the person of Jesus. They believed in His power, not necessarily His deity and purpose. Without doubt, this propensity to follow after the power of God and never seek to know Him is just as alive and well in our day. Those who truly believe in Jesus place their trust and faith in Him alone. They seek to know Him, rely upon Him, and commit their lives to Him as the divine Messiah.

Read John 6:2, 14–15, 60–66.

Questions:

What instances in Scripture can you recall when God's power was made manifest and those drawn by the miraculous soon fell away?

_____

_____

Can you think of instances in your own experience?

_____

_____

How could you effectively minister truth to such a person?

_____

_____

Behind the Scenes

Nicodemus, a Pharisee and "a ruler of the Jews" (John 3:1), wanted to meet with Jesus while He was still in Jerusalem. As a ruler of the Jews, Nicodemus was a member of the Sanhedrin—a ruling body of seventy-one scribes, elders, and priests. These men preserved and interpreted the law and were empowered to excommunicate persons who violated Jewish religious law and to try cases against false prophets and rebellious elders.

Jesus referred to Nicodemus as a "teacher of Israel" (v. 10). This could indicate that Nicodemus held an official teaching office in Israel or that he was a very prominent teacher. As such, he should have understood the Hebrew Scriptures' implicit teaching regarding spiritual rebirth and its necessity for entrance into God's kingdom. The prophets alluded to this (Ezekiel 36:22–27; 37:1–14), and many Old Testament stories illustrated it (Genesis 6:13—9:19; Exodus 14:15—15:21; 2 Kings 5:14).

Kingdom Life—*You Must Be Born Again*

Before Nicodemus even asked Jesus a question, Jesus began to speak authoritatively to him, this "ruler of the Jews" (John 3:1). He spoke to him about being "born again" (v. 3), literally "born from above." Jesus spoke of a spiritual regeneration and transformation that takes a person out of the kingdom of darkness and death and into the kingdom of light and life, also known as the kingdom of God. It is imperative that we understand the meaning of Jesus' words to Nicodemus.

Upon repentance, a new order of life opens to the believer in Jesus Christ. Jesus used the concept of "new birth" to dramatically indicate three things: (1) Without new birth there is no life and no relationship with God (John 14:6). (2) In new birth, a new perspective comes as we "see the kingdom of God" (3:3). God's Word becomes clear, and the Holy Spirit's works and wonders are believed and experienced—faith is alive. (3) Through new birth we are introduced (literally we "enter") into a new realm where God's new kingdom order can be realized (2 Corinthians 5:17). New birth is more than simply being "saved." It is a requalifying experience, opening up the possibilities of our whole being to the supernatural dimension of life and fitting us for a beginning in God's kingdom order.

Word Wealth—*Loved*

Loved: Greek *agapao* (ag-ah-pah'-o); Strong's #25: To love unconditionally, to love by choice and by an act of the will. The word denotes unconquerable benevolence and undefeatable goodwill. *Agapao* will never seek anything but the highest good for fellow humankind. *Agapao* (the verb) and *agape* (the noun) are the words associated with God's unconditional love. Such love does not need a chemistry, an affinity, or a feeling. *Agapao* is a word that exclusively belongs to the Christian community. Loving this way is virtually unknown to writers outside the New Testament—or outside the kingdom.

John 3:16

The theme of this beautiful summary of the gospel is God's love made manifest in an infinitely glorious manner. Let's take a look at the incredible message contained in these few words of Jesus.

"For God so loved the world that He gave . . ."

With the definition of *agapao* in mind, Jesus tells you that God chooses to love you. His love is not based on feeling or circumstance, but flows from Him as an expression of His nature and will. It is a love that is not earned and cannot end. In all things He seeks only to confer upon you what works for your highest good. God's love is a giving love—a love that does not depend upon your actions, attitudes, or receptivity. All that God is and does *is* love.

"His only begotten Son . . ."

"Only begotten" can also be translated "unique" and is often used interchangeably with "beloved." (See Matthew 3:17.) Jesus is the only begotten of the Father. This does not refer to Christ's earthly conception or birth but to the unique, eternal, loving relationship He has with the heavenly Father as His Son. He came to reveal the Father, and we now can behold His glory—the manifestation of God's inward being, shining like rays of sunlight showing forth the presence and power of their source, the sun. In this way Jesus revealed the magnificence of deity through His humanity.

"that whoever believes in Him . . ."

Absolutely anyone, regardless of past sin or present condition, can be the recipient of God's Gift—His only Son—and through Him enter into the kingdom of almighty God. All that is required is to be absolutely convinced, totally persuaded of the truth of His Gift of love. The same word (*pisteuo*) translated here as "believes" is translated in other places as "commit." Therefore, *pisteuo* also conveys the sense of total reliance, not just mere acknowledgment. It means to place total confidence and trust. We must entrust Jesus with our lives and our eternal destiny, having full confidence in His ability and motivation.

"should not perish . . ."

In contrast to everlasting life, this is everlasting death or destruction, which is so horrible an option that we should readily become as radical as necessary in order to avoid it (Mark 9:43–47).

"but have everlasting life."

This term implies more than simply life as we know it without end. It is a new order and totally new dimension of life bestowed from above. Although it ultimately pertains to the forever life believers will experience in heaven, it is "abundantly" present now (John 10:10), as well as being a reality that has no end (John 5:24; 10:28).

Read 1 John 4:7–16; Matthew 8:12; Romans 6:23; Jude 13.

Questions:

How do you reconcile God's abundant, unconditional love and the reality of hell?

_____

_____

_____

In what ways do you experience in day-to-day life the everlasting life Jesus promises?

_____

_____

_____

Doubt, at some level, is common to all. How can one experience doubt and continue to operate in *pisteuo*?

_____

_____

Do you understand what it means to be born again from above? Have you placed your trust in Christ and experienced the new birth, the regeneration and transformation brought about by the work of the Holy Spirit? If not, take the opportunity to do that right now, then record the date and fact of your commitment below.

_____

_____

On the other hand, if you know you have become and are now a child of God's kingdom, record here how you know that's so. It's often helpful, particularly when doubts come, to have a written record of our commitment to the King.

_____

_____

Probing the Depths

The miracle of Jesus' turning water into wine almost always raises the issue of whether it is right for Christians to drink alcohol. Some believers think that the Bible teaches (explicitly or implicitly) total abstinence, while others believe that Scripture permits moderate, though not excessive, drinking. Those Christians who accept the latter view are divided, however, with some believing that abstinence is more socially responsible in a culture where alcohol abuse is a serious problem.

Below you will find a list of relevant Bible texts in order for you to probe the depths of this question. Discover for yourself what the Bible has to say on this controversial topic.

- **Alcohol's Use:** Genesis 14:18; 27:28; Exodus 22:29; 29:38–41; Numbers 15:6–10; 28:11–15; Deuteronomy 14:26; Ruth 2:14; 1 Samuel 25:18; 2 Samuel 16:1–2; Nehemiah 5:18; Psalm 104:14–15; Proverbs 9:4–6; 25:20; 31:6–7; Ecclesiastes 2:24; 9:7; Song of Solomon 5:1; Isaiah 25:6; 55:1–2; Joel 2:23–24; 3:17–18; Amos 9:13; Matthew 11:19; 26:27–29; 27:48; Mark 2:14–17, 22; 14:23–25; Luke 5:27–39; 7:34; 10:33–34; 22:17–18, 20; John 2:3–11; 1 Corinthians 11:23–26; 1 Timothy 5:23.

- **Alcohol's Abuse:** Genesis 9:20–24; 19:30–38; Deuteronomy 21:20–21; 1 Samuel 1:13–16; 25:36–37; Job 12:25; Proverbs 20:1; 21:17; 23:17–21, 29–35; 31:4–5; Isaiah 5:11, 22; 19:14; 28:7–8; 56:12; Jeremiah 25:27–29; 48:26; 51:39–40; Hosea 4:11; 7:5; Joel 1:5; Amos 6:1, 6; Habakkuk 2:5, 15–16; Luke 21:34; Romans 13:13; 1 Corinthians 5:11; 6:9–10; 11:20–21, 27–32; Galatians 5:19–21; Ephesians 5:18; 1 Timothy 3:2–3, 8; Titus 1:7; 2:3; 1 Peter 4:3.

- **Alcohol Restrictions:** Leviticus 10:8–11; Numbers 6:1–4, 13–20; Deuteronomy 29:5–6; Judges 13:3–5, 7, 13–14; Jeremiah 35; Ezekiel 44:15, 21; Daniel 1:8–16; Matthew 11:18; Luke 1:13–15; 7:33; Ephesians 5:18; 1 Timothy 3:2–3, 8; Titus 1:7; 2:3.

- **Related Principles:** Romans 14; 1 Corinthians 6:12; 10:31; Galatians 5:22–23; Philippians 2:3–4; 1 Timothy 4:1–5; 6:17; Titus 1:15; 2 Peter 1:5–11.

Kingdom Life—*Worship in Spirit and Truth*

In Jesus' exchange with the Samaritan woman, she attempted to take the conversation in a different direction by bringing up a controversial topic for her day and time—where to worship. Jesus' answer defines true worship.

It does not matter where one worships. What is of prime importance is the attitude of heart and mind. True worship is not mere form and ceremony but spiritual reality that is in harmony with the nature of God, who is Spirit. Worship must also be in truth, that is, transparent, sincere, and according to biblical mandates.

It is the believer's responsibility to discover how the Lord wants to be worshipped and to explore and cultivate a relationship with Him out of which sincere, Holy Spirit–enabled worship will flow. Jesus tells us to worship in "spirit" (John 4:23). This is a worship that is alive through new birth and aglow with Holy Spirit enablement. Worship is not a mechanical, rote, or merely human activity, but dynamically capacitated spiritual action. Jesus also tells us to worship in "truth" (v. 23). This emphasizes biblical integrity joined to personal honesty, a sincere heart, a transparent manner, and a relational integrity. Meaning and being what we say, as well as being spiritually energized in our worship, opens the way to true worship—the worship the Father seeks.

Record Your Thoughts

The primary messages of John's gospel are in regard to Jesus' relationship to God and our relationship to Jesus. At this point in our study, it would be beneficial for you to take an honest look at your relationship with Jesus and list your areas of struggle. As you list each one, try to locate a Bible passage containing an answer to that struggle. Take each struggle to the Lord and ask Him to lead you and enable you to embrace that answer as you continue in your study of living beyond the ordinary. Yours truly can be an extraordinary life!

_____

_____

_____

SESSION FOUR

Living Water

John 4:1–54

Kingdom Key—He Quenches Our Thirst

Revelation 21:6 I will give of the fountain of the water of life freely to him who thirsts.

If you have ever known true thirst, that dry, parched, scratchy feeling that demands relief, then you know the compelling quest for relief and the incredible joy that cool, clear water can bring. It's like falling into a sparkling pool following a workout on a scorching-hot summer day.

What's true about our insatiable physical thirst is also true about our spiritual thirst—that parched ground within us all, longing to be drenched with the never-ending waters of ultimate purpose, meaning, forgiveness, redemption, renewal. In the gospel of John we learn about a drink that has no equal. Once you taste it, once you let it touch the tongue of your soul, it will flood your entire being until you stand fully soaked for an eternity.

You're about to find out about the ultimate thirst quencher—the only drink that never needs replenishing, the only one that can satisfy your soul forever.

Read Psalms 1; 42:1–2; 63:1; Revelation 22:17.

Questions:

Do you have an insatiable thirst for the things of the Lord?

_____

_____

_____

Why do you believe this is so?

✎ _____

_____

What are the similarities between water and the benefits of the kingdom?

✎ _____

_____

What can be gained by drinking deeply of kingdom water?

✎ _____

_____

Traveling Orders

While Jesus and His disciples were carrying on a baptism ministry in Judea, Jesus learned that the Pharisees had gotten wind of the fact that His ministry was baptizing more people than John the Baptist's was. So this led Jesus to pull up stakes, pack His tent, and start off for Galilee (John 4:1–3).

Several times throughout this study, we'll see Jesus leaving a place or a group at just the right time. He always seemed to know when it was time to move on. And He always knew the route from which the most glory would ensue.

Samaria was typically avoided by Jews even though traveling through it made the trip between Judea and Galilee much easier. The Samaritans were a mixed race—a product of Israelites' intermarrying with Assyrians. The Jews did not socialize with the Samaritans because Jews would be made unclean by sharing eating or drinking vessels with Samaritans. But Jesus needed to go through Samaria.

How often does the Spirit of God prompt us that it is time to move, only to have us dig in our heels and refuse? Or how often are we prompted to go a certain direction and allow our logical minds to convince us of an alternate route? Our own opinions and our own fears can rob us of incredible journeys with the Lord. But it is necessary that we listen *and* obey.

Read Proverbs 3:5–6.

Questions:

In the times you have failed to follow the Spirit's prompting as to when or where to move, what have been the results?

✎_____

_____

With this in mind, what do you now hear in Jesus' command, "Follow Me" (John 1:43)?

✎_____

_____

 Behind the Scenes

You can't understand the antagonism that existed between first-century Jews and Samaritans without knowing some history.

God had chosen Jerusalem as the worship center for Israel. It was built on Mount Moriah where Abraham had offered Isaac (Genesis 22:2), and it was the site where the temple had finally been built by Solomon (2 Chronicles 3:1–2). Jerusalem was definitely the Holy City (Jeremiah 3:17; Zechariah 14:16).

But when Israel split into two kingdoms (931 B.C.), Jerusalem was located in Judah, the Southern Kingdom. The ruler of the Northern Kingdom, Jeroboam, wanted to ensure that the people in his domain didn't shift their allegiance to Rehoboam, the ruler of the Southern Kingdom (Judah), after traveling to Jerusalem to worship (1 Kings 12:27). So Jeroboam established golden-calf worship centers in the north and instituted a substitute feast for Jerusalem's Passover, which continued until the Northern Kingdom fell to the Assyrians in 722 B.C.

Samaria, as part of the Northern Kingdom, blended their tainted worship of God with the religious beliefs and practices of the conquering Assyrians. The result was an idolatrous hybrid form of worship practiced by the Samaritans.

When the exiled Israelites began returning to their homeland (539 B.C.), they were appalled by the compromises the Samaritans had made with the foreign settlers, so the returning Jews would not allow the Samaritans to participate in the rebuilding of the temple in Jerusalem

(Ezra 4:1–3). This exacerbated the division between the two groups (vv. 4–5; Nehemiah 4:1–2) and eventually led to the Samaritans' building their own temple on Mount Gerizim in Samaria, which was later burned by the Jewish leader John Hyrcanus in 128 B.C.

Behind the Scenes

In first-century Jewish culture, as in most of the world, women were not held in appropriate esteem. Samaritan women, as far as Jewish prejudice was concerned, were even further down the acceptability scale. To drink from a Samaritan woman's vessel resulted in one's becoming ceremonially unclean. Jesus ignored these perceptions and thereby challenged the racial and religious bigotry of His time.

Kingdom Life—*Love the Unlovely*

Jesus' choice to go through Samaria speaks of an overriding intentionality. He was compelled by the Spirit to take a direction based on unconditional love, not racial bigotry. Jesus frequently broke the mold of religious acceptability and reached with love toward the tax collectors, sinners, and those the religious considered unworthy of notice.

Jesus gave time and energy to relationships, which sometimes meant experiencing pain and loss. In the exchange with the Samaritan woman, Jesus gives us a life quality to emulate: He calls us to enter intentionally and sensitively into the experiences of others, bringing His light and love to bear. We are to reach out in love to all those who do not yet know truth and to those who express it differently.

Read Matthew 22:34–40; 1 John 4:7–16; 1 Corinthians 13:1–13.

Questions:

With what people groups or certain types of people do you have difficulty associating?

_____

_____

Why do you believe this is so?

_____

_____

How can you reach out in love to those who are deceived spiritually without judgment or condemnation?

✎_____

_____

How can theological or doctrinal differences be handled so as to promote unity in the body of Christ?

✎_____

_____

Kingdom Life—*An Empowered Witness*

Considering the ongoing contempt of Jews for Samaritans, the reputation of the Samaritan woman, and the cultural restriction of male and female interaction, this scenario becomes a classic lesson in God's redemptive action. Jesus' initiative forgives, restores, and empowers a woman, who then persuades others to heed a Jewish Messiah!

Our Savior's grace, seen in this woman of Samaria, illustrates how past overt or covert prejudices, beliefs, practices, and exposures need not confine or destroy the potential of a person. A transformed woman became a great evangelistic influence as many Samaritans responded to Jesus as Messiah. An added lesson of significance is to see the Savior reaching out to those deemed different or indifferent, teaching the value of affirming the worth of all people. An unnamed Samaritan woman received life-changing revelation that had eluded many rabbinical scholars—spiritual insight that propelled her to another dimension, perceiving Jesus as "a prophet" (John 4:19), and then as "the Christ" (v. 29). She is a model of how true revelation may translate into a powerful witness.

Read Mark 16:15; Isaiah 43:10–12; Psalm 40:8–10.

Questions:

Has the Lord ever required you to move in an unexpected way that resulted in glory to His name? What was the circumstance and outcome?

✎_____

_____

_____

In what ways do you find it difficult to be a witness for the Lord in word as well as deed?

✎ _____

_____

_____

Have you ever had the joy of being instrumental in the salvation of another? What were the circumstances? How did you overcome the hesitancies you listed above?

✎ _____

_____

_____

Word Wealth—*Savior*

Savior: Greek *soter* (so-tare'); Strong's *#4990*: This word designates a deliverer, preserver, savior, benefactor, rescuer. It is used to describe both God the Father and Jesus the Son. It shares the same Greek root word as *sozo*, "to save," and *soteria*, "salvation."

The Purpose of Signs and Wonders

The healing of the nobleman's son not only demonstrates Jesus' power to heal, but it underscores the principle that He did not regard signs and wonders as ends in themselves. Rather, they were intended to bring the recipients of the miracle to faith in Jesus as the Christ.

No one will ever experience the continual flow of "living water" (John 4:10) through signs and wonders. Those signs and wonders are to create within us the thirst that causes us to seek hard after God.

Read Isaiah 55:1; Matthew 10:8.

Questions:

Do you experience this flow of living water in your life?

✎ _____

_____

What hinders this experience?

✎ _____

_____

_____

In what ways can others benefit from this flow?

✎ _____

_____

_____

What steps can you take to increase this flow in your life?

✎ _____

_____

_____

Record Your Thoughts

Questions:

Have you ever attempted to quench your thirst through things of the earth rather than through the Lord? How? What was the outcome?

✎ _____

_____

_____

Do you experience dry seasons in your walk with the Lord? What do you believe causes these?

✎ _____

_____

_____

What steps can you take to bring back the rain/reign?

✎ _____

_____

_____

SESSION FIVE

Know the Father

John 5:1–47

Kingdom Key—*We Are in His Image*

Genesis 1:27 God created man in His own image; in the image of God He created him; male and female He created them.

God created us in His image. What this means is that we *resemble* and *represent* our Creator. Like Him, we can think, feel, choose, act, refrain, develop relationships, love, and create. In these ways we resemble Him. We represent Him through our stewardship over the earth; our authority to enter into covenants with each other, as well as with Him, our responsibilities to execute justice, rule, and serve; and our privilege to be ambassadors to the world, spreading the gospel of Christ by the power of His Holy Spirit and making disciples.

Read James 3:9.

Questions:

Why is it important that we remain conscious of the fact that we represent God to a lost, unbelieving world?

_____

_____

In what ways do you succeed in representing Him?

_____

_____

In what ways do you fail to do so?

_____

_____

Word Wealth—*Image*

Image: Hebrew *tselem* (tseh'-lem); Strong's #6754: This word signifies a representative figure. It conveys the idea of carrying the essential nature of the original. Man was created both male and female, intended for loving unity with more than one person, in the image of the triune God.

Kingdom Life—*Jesus Reveals the Father*

Like our Creator, one of the greatest powers we have is the power to create. We can bring into existence art, technology, concepts—all kinds of ideas and goods meant to benefit human beings. We can also create something more intimate, more valuable, indeed, of eternal value: other human beings. In our own image, we produce sons and daughters (Genesis 5:1–3), give them names, food, and clothes; we educate them and set them on their own to repeat the process. They resemble and represent us. They look, sound, think, and even feel like us. They also carry on our values, perspectives, and names. When others see them, they believe our children stand for who we are and what we've done. Sometimes our children make us feel proud; at other times we wish we could fire them and hire replacements.

Our heavenly Father has a Son—an eternal, uncreated Son, but a Son who is identical to Him. His Son resembles and represents Him with utter perfection, so the Father is always pleased with Him. Consequently, when we see Jesus, His Son, we can see the Father shining through.

So let's look more closely at Jesus. He'll show us the Father we can't see or touch.

Read John 12:44–45; 14:8–9.

Questions:

What qualities or attributes of God does Jesus reveal to us?

_____

_____

Do you view God as Jesus revealed Him?

_____

_____

What aspects of God's nature seem outside your experience?

✎ _____

_____

Why do you believe this is so?

✎ _____

_____

 Behind the Scenes

John 5 opens with Jesus in Jerusalem to attend an unnamed Jewish feast. There He passes by the pool of Bethesda (meaning "Place of Outpouring" or "House of Grace"). This pool was actually twin pools large enough to swim in. They may have been filled partly from the great reservoirs of Solomon's Pools (which were southwest of Bethlehem) and partly from an intermittent spring that periodically stirred up the water.

Do You Want to Be Healed?

The first step in overcoming problems, whether they are physical, emotional, or spiritual, is to admit you are in need and desire a change. Jesus asked the man who had been lying by the Bethesda pool for thirty-eight years a very important question: "Do you want to be made well?" (John 5:6). In other words, do you care enough about your problem to do something about it—even if it requires on your part some action, effort, sacrifice, or even suffering?

As is typical of so many in need, this man answered the Lord with self-pity. When Jesus sees you need help and sends a willing person to help, do you play the martyr role? "There's no hope for me. Nobody loves me." The person who clings to this attitude is unlikely to experience healing.

Because Jesus is gracious and knows your deepest desires, He often cuts through your weeping and self-martyrdom and puts you to the test. "Get up," He says. "Take your problem and move on. Do not wait for other people to pity you. Get up."

If you are in need of a touch from the Lord, ask yourself if you are eager enough to be changed that you are willing to do something about your situation. When you let God know you are obedient to His will and eager to do whatever it takes for you to be whole, He will send Jesus in the form of a person, a verse from His Word, or a new thought in your mind. Act upon what God tells you to do. He made you, and He knows how to fix precisely what is broken within you.

Finally, when you feel God's power bring about positive changes in your life, do not let doubters convince you of any other source. Walk firmly away, as did the man with his mat under his arm, and say simply, "Jesus healed me." It is through God's healing touch that we show forth His glory and are made ever more in His image.

Read James 4.

Questions:

Out of all the hurting people seeking to get well around the pool of Bethesda, why do you think Jesus chose only this one person to heal?

_____

_____

In what ways have you seen, in yourself or others, the desire to hold on to the familiar rather than trust God for healing and freedom?

_____

_____

How can pride be at the root of this problem?

_____

_____

What other sinful attitudes and motivations result in failure to seek healing?

_____

_____

What steps can be taken to combat these tendencies in your own life?

_____

_____

_____

Behind the Scenes

The words "waiting for the moving of the water" (John 5:3) through the end of verse 4 are absent from all extant copies of John's gospel until A.D. 400. For this reason many Bible scholars see this section of John 5 as a copyist's explanatory insertion, not as part of the original, God-inspired text. However, the rest of the narrative makes clear that there was nonetheless an unusual presence at work there on occasion (v. 7). Although such copying insertions have occurred over the years during the transmission of the Scriptures, they are innocent of dishonest intent (as with this explanatory phrase), and none of them affect any key issue of Christian doctrine.

Kingdom Extra

For more about how the Scriptures were transmitted over the centuries, including how scholars can tell what material was part of the original text, you may find the following sources helpful: *A General Introduction to the Bible,* by Norman L. Geisler and William E. Nix, rev. ed. (Chicago, IL: Moody Press, 1986); *From Ancient Tablets to Modern Translations: A General Introduction to the Bible,* by David Ewert (Grand Rapids, MI: Zondervan Publishing House, 1983).

Kingdom Life—*Know God's Healing Power*

In order that the church's mission might not be limited to the abilities of mere human enterprise, the Holy Spirit provides specially designed, distributed, and energized gifts. Among them are "gifts of healings" (1 Corinthians 12:9, 28, 30). The clear intent is that the supernatural healing of the sick should be a permanent ministry established in the church alongside and abetting the work of evangelizing the world. This gift is for today—timeless—for "the gifts and the calling of God are irrevocable" (Romans 11:29).

Read Isaiah 53:4–5; Mark 1:40–45.

Questions:

In what ways have you experienced supernatural physical, psychological, or emotional healing?

_____

Have you had an instance when a loved one was not healed? What happened? How did you feel about it?

✎_____

_____

What reasons can you discover for unanswered prayer for healing?

✎_____

_____

Why should or should not one preface prayer with, "If it be Your will"?

✎_____

_____

Probing the Depths

Jesus said that He did only those things He saw the Father do (John 5:19). He did not act independently of the Father. Though He is God, He humbled Himself and became obedient even to death.

If Jesus, the eternal Word, one in being with the Father, acted only as He saw the Father act, acted only as led by God Almighty, should we do any less?

Too often, prayer is seen as a forum for demand based on God's Word; or an opportunity to share a wish list; or a last resort when all else has failed; or even as a duty to be performed. True prayer is a communion of hearts. It is aligning ourselves with the heart of God in a matter: "Your kingdom come. Your will be done on earth as it is in heaven" (Matthew 6:10).

Read Philippians 2:5–11; James 4:3; John 14:12–18.

Questions:

What attitude of heart do these Scriptures reveal in Jesus?

✎_____

_____

How might you come into full realization of God's heart in order to pray more effectively?

✎ _____

_____

Immediately following Jesus' assurance that "greater works" (John 14:12) will be done by believers, He tells of the coming Holy Spirit. If prayer is a communion of hearts, what role does the Spirit play in submitted prayer?

✎ _____

_____

Kingdom Life—*Jesus Is Lord*

John 5:17–47 records Jesus' words as He proclaimed His relationship to the Father and the purpose of His ministry on earth. This entire discourse is addressed to those who accused Him of blasphemy. While His desire is for them to be saved, their problem is not that they cannot believe, but that they are unwilling to accept His offer of life. His love for them is made clear, even in the midst of His statements regarding the cost of unbelief.

Few people, regardless of belief structure or worldview, would disagree that Jesus was a good man, maybe even a prophet. Others call Him Lord. If He is not Lord, then He was neither a prophet nor a good man.

If Jesus is not the only begotten Son of God, the long-prophesied Messiah, then He was an incredibly prolific, convincing liar or a raving lunatic. There are no other choices. No sane person believes themselves to be God. And no sane person would propagate a lie that would surely lead to death, not to mention that no manufactured lies could stand the test of time and the scrutiny of generations as has Jesus' proclamation that He is the Messiah.

Read John 8:54–58.

Questions:

Why did Jesus use the term "I AM" (John 8:58)?

✎ _____

_____

What truths are contained in this statement?

✎ _____

_____

_____

What other Scriptures can you locate that record Jesus' own words in regard to His identity and His mission?

✎ _____

_____

_____

What does it mean to say, "Jesus is Lord"?

✎ _____

_____

_____

A Case for Divine Equality

Jesus was never one to back down, especially when He wanted to make a point that His audience desperately needed to hear and understand. So, in the face of a lynch-mob mentality, Jesus laid out some of the most direct and challenging teaching the people had heard from Him so far. Jesus answered the charge that He claimed to be "equal with God" (John 5:18). He gave the Jews several reasons to accept His claim to deity. Outline Jesus' answer (John 8:54–58) below, restating each of His reasons and the support He gave for each.

HIS REASONS	HIS EVIDENCE
✎ _____	_____
_____	_____
_____	_____
_____	_____
_____	_____

Record Your Thoughts

God made us in His image because He desired fellowship with us. He gave us minds, wills, emotions, imaginations—all the things that separate man from beast. He wanted us to be able to choose to know and love Him, and only a creature endowed with those godly attributes could choose, know, or love.

Although man's relationship with God ceased to be personal and became distant and law-ridden, God provided a way to recapture that fellowship for which He made us, that bond of unity. If we believe Jesus is the Christ and receive the new life He gives, the possibility of a close personal relationship with God has been reinstated.

Questions:

Prayer is an outgrowth of your relationship with God. Why is this a true statement?

_____

_____

_____

With this concept of prayer in mind, what does your prayer life say about your relationship with God?

_____

_____

_____

What truth contained in this session has most impacted you and why?

_____

_____

_____

With which aspect of this session do you struggle most?

_____

_____

_____

SESSION SIX

An Unveiled Reality

John 6:1–71

Kingdom Key—*Called Outside Our Comfort Zone*

Luke 12:51 Do you suppose that I came to give peace on earth? I tell you, not at all, but rather division.

Jesus has been given many labels by friends and enemies alike. Hardly anyone lacks an opinion, and for good reason. History has never seen such a one as Jesus of Nazareth. From His conception in the womb of a virgin to His ascension into heaven to reign with the Father as Lord of the universe, Jesus' earthly life has raised eyebrows and voices, created heroes and martyrs, provided inspiration and cause for debate, and created division within families, communities, and even nations. No other leader has had such an incredible impact on so many people for so long.

He was multifaceted and controversial. At the same time, He was deeply loved and just as deeply hated. Sometimes His message was so clear that everyone understood what He said. At other times, however, not even His closest followers tracked with Him. His teaching was pointed, practical, and often hard to handle, and His miracles didn't always lead to high rankings in popularity contests. Jesus was a disturbing figure.

John 6 reveals this Jesus in some of His complexity. It shows Him doing great wonders, but it also shows Him presenting some troubling teaching. Friend and foe alike are seen struggling with Him, just as they do today. Truth does that to us, doesn't it? It rarely leaves us comfortable. So let's press beyond our comfort zones and discover what awaits us in the sixth chapter of John's gospel.

Read Matthew 10:34–39; Revelation 1:12–16.

Questions:

How do you reconcile Jesus' being the "Prince of Peace" (Isaiah 9:6) and His words about bringing division?

✎ _____

_____

Have you experienced a breach in a relationship as a result of your faith?

✎ _____

_____

Have you ever been called to end a relationship because of your love for Jesus?

✎ _____

_____

 Kingdom Life—*Faith Will Be Tested*

Apart from the resurrection, the feeding of the five thousand is the only miracle recorded in all four gospels. Obviously, it was an event that left an indelible impression on those present. Jesus chose this opportunity to test Philip's faith.

Jesus asked Philip a question that contained much more than a simple request for information. It was of no consequence to Jesus that the cost of feeding five thousand men (that does not count the women and children present) was equivalent to eight months' wages. What was of great importance to Jesus was Philip's faith. Jesus intimated the impossible and gave Philip the opportunity to recognize and embrace His ability to overcome any obstacle. Philip responded by stating physical fact and ignoring the spiritual possibilities.

How often do we find ourselves in the same struggle with physical reality? We see situations that are beyond our meager abilities and fall into despair.

When our faith is tested, we must remember that Jesus is not dependent upon physical realities, nor is He bound by them. What is impossible in the natural does not limit what God can accomplish in our lives. He is above all things and more powerful than any circumstance.

Read Romans 5:1–5; James 1:2–4; Hebrews 11:1–6.

Questions:

It is often said that faith is a verb. Why do you believe this is so?

_____

_____

When has your faith and/or character ever been tested?

_____

_____

What were the circumstances and the outcome?

_____

_____

What did you learn about yourself and God as a result?

_____

_____

When circumstance causes faith to falter, what are the results?

_____

_____

Why can we not please God without faith?

_____

_____

In your own words, what are the purposes of trial and tribulation?

_____

_____

Why do you think that, among all the miracles Jesus performed (excluding His resurrection), this one is the only miracle recorded in all four Gospels? What makes this miracle so significant?

Behind the Scenes

Passover was one of three feasts in Jewish tradition requiring a pilgrimage to Jerusalem. (The other two were Pentecost, marking the day God gave Moses the Ten Commandments, and the Feast of Tabernacles, in remembrance of the Israelites' forty years of wandering in the wilderness.)

God visited ten catastrophic plagues upon Egypt for refusing to release Israel from captivity. The last plague was the death of all the firstborn. Israelites were instructed to mark their doorposts with the blood of a lamb. When the angel of death passed over, those homes so marked would be spared. Following this last plague, Israel was released from captivity and began their journey to the promised land. Passover commemorates the Israelites' deliverance from the angel of death when the last plague was visited upon Egypt.

For the duration of Passover, no leavened bread was to be eaten. Thus it is also referred to as the Feast of Unleavened Bread.

Kingdom Life—*See Him as He Is*

Although the disciples walked daily with Jesus, they could not grasp His true identity and His ultimate purpose. Their concept of Jesus was as an earthly ruler with limited power. In walking on the water, Jesus revealed His supreme authority over all things. He demonstrated to them that His existence was beyond the physical realm, and His being beyond the human condition.

As the waves and wind pounded their boat, the disciples feared their circumstances. When they saw Jesus on the sea, they most likely feared for the safety of their Master. Their fear was relieved when they welcomed Jesus.

In our attitudes, actions, and responses, we also impose upon the Lord earthly limitations. Whenever fear or anxiety overtakes us, we have ceased to recognize His true identity and have attempted to relegate Him to a position of powerlessness over our reality. This is not the case, dear one. Jesus is not limited by anything or anyone. He is all in all. Through Him all that exists is held together. In Him we have our being.

When we look beyond the storms in our lives to see Jesus and welcome Him into our boat, we will find peace. The storm will cease to blow our lives about, and we will soon find that we have passed safely through the storm to continue our journey.

Read Isaiah 43:1–2; Mark 4:35–41.

Questions:

When have you experienced anxiety or fear?

_____

_____

What was your reaction?

_____

_____

What was the outcome of the fearful situation?

_____

_____

What have you learned from this experience?

_____

_____

How has your view of God changed as a result?

_____

_____

 Kingdom Life—*He Is the Living Bread*

From John 6:22 to the end of the chapter, Jesus reveals a great deal about who He is, His mission, and what people can receive from Him. One of His revelations, "a hard saying" (v. 60), leads to a significant drop in the numbers of His followers. They did not understand the meaning of Jesus' words and were repulsed by their perceived meaning.

This lengthy section provides us with the most in-depth New Testament explanation of the significance of communion and how it is vastly more than a mere ordinance commemorating Jesus' death.

The gospel of John contains seven "I am" statements of Jesus. Here we find the first: "I am the bread of life" (6:35). He makes this pronouncement three times in this passage. He wanted to impress upon us that He is the real heavenly bread, the true, life-sustaining power. Read Psalm 105:40–45.

Questions:

What are the similarities between the Bread of Life and the manna God provided the Israelites?

✎ _____

_____

What are the differences?

✎ _____

_____

Do you tend to depend on manna from God or the Bread of Life?

✎ _____

_____

Kingdom Extra

Before pressing on, read back through John 6:25–71 and record the "I am" sayings of Jesus, the statements He prefaced with "I am." Then indicate what you think these sayings tell us about who Jesus is. In the fourth gospel, all the "I am" sayings play a very important role. We'll look at them more closely later in this study.

✎ _____

_____

Probing the Depths

Jesus' "hard saying" (John 6:60) is indeed hard. His words about eating His flesh and drinking His blood have been interpreted a variety of ways by Christians throughout the centuries.

Some see His words as referring to the Eucharist or Lord's Supper. And among those who do, four views have been held. One is called *transubstantiation,* and it is embraced by Roman Catholicism. It teaches that in a mysterious way the bread and drink of the Eucharist really become Jesus' body and blood.

A second view, *consubstantiation,* is common among Lutherans, and it says that Jesus' body and blood are present in, with, and under the eucharistic elements of bread and wine, but they do not turn into these elements.

The third position is the *spiritual* view, which many Protestant Reformers accept. It sees Jesus' flesh-and-blood teaching as symbolic or metaphorical, indicating that through the elements of the Eucharist, Christ's presence and our union with Him are manifest spiritually, not physically or materially.

The *memorial* view, which is held by many Protestants, takes Jesus' words as a parallel to the Jewish Passover Feast. Both meals—the Lord's Supper and the Passover—are meals of remembrance, celebrated to remind believers of what God has done to save them and to participate by faith in the present power of the covenant relationship represented in the rite.

A fifth position, held by some Catholics as well as Protestants, could be called the *way-to-salvation* view. It proposes that Jesus' words about eating His flesh and drinking His blood are parallel to and carry the same meaning as seeing and believing in Him in order to receive eternal life (John 6:40). Consequently, from this viewpoint, Jesus' words in John 6 have nothing to do with the Lord's Supper; they are merely another way of telling people how they can be saved.

Interpretations vary, but given the weight Jesus placed on these words, we should settle the matter with spiritual discernment and sensitivity, emphasizing the spiritual meaning, as Jesus said (6:63).

Record Your Thoughts

Questions:

What are your own views in regard to communion or the Lord's Supper?

✎ _____

_____

_____

Tell in your own words what it means that Jesus is the Bread of Life.

✎ _____

_____

_____

In preparation for the remainder of this study, locate the other six "I am" statements of Jesus in the gospel of John.

✎ _____

_____

_____

What impact does each of these statements have on your life?

✎ _____

_____

_____

On the Defense

John 7:1—8:59

Kingdom Key—*Depend on the Author*

Hebrews 12:1–2 Let us lay aside every weight, and the sin which so easily ensnares us, and let us run with endurance the race that is set before us, looking unto Jesus, the author and finisher of our faith, who for the joy that was set before Him endured the cross, despising the shame, and has sat down at the right hand of the throne of God.

There once was an author who created a whole world in his mind. The landscape, colors, smells, sights: everything about this world had his fingerprints. Even its creatures, great and small, reflected him in some way. He wrote freethinkers into this world. These were higher creatures with great potential.

One day, while he was writing the story about this world, he decided to become part of the story, so he wrote himself into it. He made himself like one of the higher creatures. Remaining inconspicuous for a while, he observed the world he had created firsthand. The trees, animals, sea life, sky, and other aspects of the natural world were even more beautiful and harmonious to his eyes than his words had described. On the other hand, the freethinkers were having trouble getting along with each other and their surroundings. In fact, they disagreed with one another far more than there were issues to dispute over. This upset the author, so he decided to do something about it.

Picking just the right moment, he introduced himself to a prestigious gathering of the Freethinkers High Society. He told them that he was their author, their creator, and that he would be delighted to help them resolve their differences. But they would not believe him and scoffed at his claims.

"I told you," he said, "I gave birth to you. At one time you were just a part of my imagination. But I gave you life. I put pen to paper and brought you into being. Now I would like to create some solutions for you." His offer was met with disbelief, anger, and arrogance. They did not believe he could be their creator.

"Oh, but I assure you I am who I say I am," the author said. But no matter what proof he provided, only a few of the Freethinkers would believe him, and those were ostracized from the Freethinkers High Society. The author's world had rejected him and his defense.

And so it is with Jesus. He is the Author. He is the beginning and the end of the story. Yet He was and is "despised and rejected by men" (Isaiah 53:3).

Read Isaiah 53:3; Philippians 2:5–11; Hebrews 2:14–18.

Questions:

What does it mean that Jesus is the author and finisher of your faith?

_____

_____

How should this affect your day-to-day experience of life with regard to anxiety and worry?

_____

_____

What difference would the continual realization of Jesus' experience of walking as a man make on your ability to trust Him?

_____

_____

Behind the Scenes

The Feast of Tabernacles (also known as the Feast of Booths) is a thanksgiving harvest festival that occurs at the end of September and the beginning of October. It also commemorates the divine guidance granted to the Israelites during the nation's wandering in the wilderness. During the festival the people erected and lived in temporary shelters made of palm and other tree branches.

Each day during the feast, a joyous celebration was observed in which the priests brought water (symbolizing the water supplied from the rock in Exodus 17) to the temple from the pool of Siloam in a golden pitcher. During the procession the people recited Isaiah 12:3. The water was poured out on the altar as an offering to God, while the people shouted and sang.

Jesus was the fulfillment of all that the ceremony typified.

Read 1 Corinthians 10:4.

Questions:

What Scripture passages can you locate wherein the living water of Jesus is mentioned?

_____

_____

What are the qualities of this living water?

_____

_____

What does it give to those who drink of it?

_____

_____

Kingdom Life—*Stand Firm*

Jesus was scoffed at and ridiculed by religious authorities, family, and strangers. But He was so confident of the Father's will for Him that He could stand firm in the face of the challenges from unbelievers, even when those challenges came from loved ones.

As the Author, Jesus is writing our story, even as we live it. There is no plot twist or mysterious element of which He is unaware. He is developing our character through each of life's pages and knows exactly who and what we are. All our tomorrows are safely hidden in the heart of the One who writes our story. Even if we veer from the intended course of the Author, He can and will always write (right) us back to the path to life.

Because of this, we, too, can stand confidently in the midst of challenge and personal attack. We need only to trust in the Author's wisdom and His never-failing love. Our identity, our purpose, our course, and our destiny are found in Him. We can stand firm in the face of any adversity, for the Author knows.

Read Acts 17:26–28; Romans 8:27–30.

Questions:

With this analogy in mind, what can you conclude about doubt, fear, or unbelief?

_____

_____

What other Scriptures can you locate that give further insight into standing firm in the face of adversity?

_____

_____

When in your life has a challenge caused you to question the Lord and/or your standing with Him?

_____

_____

What steps can you take to guard against this in the future?

_____

_____

Kingdom Extra

Jesus often likened kingdom life to water. He told the Samaritan woman about the fountain of living water. In John 7:38 He speaks of "rivers of living water."

John interprets these words of Jesus to refer to the pouring out of the Holy Spirit that was still to come. The Holy Spirit exists through all eternity but was not present at this time in the sense this verse indicates.

Those who are satisfied by receiving the fountain of water from Jesus (symbolizing new birth) will themselves become channels of spiritual refreshment for others. This fountain springs eternal so that they will never thirst again in the spiritual sense. The coming of the Holy Spirit will so fill the believer that the life-giving water of the kingdom will pour forth, leading others to discover living water and the overflowing fullness of the Spirit-filled life.

Read Revelation 21:6; 22:17.

Questions:

What qualities exist in water that give further insight into this analogy?

_____

_____

Is your life a source of living water for those around you?

_____

_____

Why do you believe this is so?

_____

_____

 Kingdom Life—*Jesus Is Our Defense*

The Pharisees and other religious leaders wanted nothing more than to trap Jesus in sin, falsehood, or unbiblical dealings. They set numerous traps for Him and each attempt failed.

When they caught a Jewish woman in the act of adultery, they again saw an opportunity to entrap Jesus in a dilemma. The offense required stoning under the law. Jesus, knowing the heart of the law and not held captive by the letter of the law, questioned their right to judge another. He then set the woman free.

We all stand guilty—caught in the act. But Jesus offers forgiveness as freely as He did with the adulterous woman.

Read Romans 8:31–39; Hebrews 7:25; 1 John 1:8–10; 2:1; James 5:16.

Questions:

Are there areas of sin in your life that remain even today?

_____

_____

What prevents you from confessing and being freed from this sin?

_____

_____

Is there someone in your life who can help you walk toward freedom in this area?

_____

_____

 Kingdom Life—*He Is the Light of the World*

Jesus, in the second of His seven "I am" statements in the gospel of John, proclaims Himself "the light of the world" (John 8:12). This statement immediately follows Jesus' compassionate interchange with the adulterous woman.

Light pierces and eliminates darkness. It may be said that light has preeminence or authority over darkness. We determined earlier that darkness represents the sinful condition of man. Therefore, Jesus' timing speaks clearly that He has the right, the authority, and the power to remove the penalty of sin.

You may wish to review Session One, Kingdom Life—*The Light of Men*, at this point.

Record Your Thoughts

Questions:

Read John 8:31–32. With these words of Jesus in mind, what truths in this session do you find the most freeing?

_____

_____

What steps do you plan to make to enable you to stand strong in the Lord?

✎_____

_____

_____

What does it mean to you that Jesus is your defense?

✎_____

_____

_____

Believing Is Seeing
John 9:1—10:39

Kingdom Key—*Desire Truth*

Isaiah 42:18 Hear, you deaf; and look, you blind, that you may see.

Throughout life, we all tend to create truths according to our own faulty perceptions rather than according to reality. A child hears parental direction, its justification, and the consequences of disobedience, yet chooses to disregard. This condition begins with toddlers and continues throughout adolescence. When asked why direction was not followed, children respond with some form of "I don't know."

Although a child may not be aware of his or her true motivation, an adolescent will often give voice to the doubt that adults really know much of anything. "You just don't understand," or "Things are different now," can be heard in just about any home containing a teenager.

Adulthood does not cure this condition. Adults may actually advance this condition to new stages of absurdity. We become more adept at rationalizing away very good reasons and clear explanations for accepting or rejecting certain ideas, positions, or behaviors. We advance beyond "I don't know" and give reasons for rejecting what we are told, even when those reasons have no supporting evidence. Too often we make choices based on denial, lies, or rationalizations and refuse to see the truth.

Why can't we just be honest and say, "I don't want to do it," or "I refuse to believe that"? Very simply, we often aren't honest with ourselves because our sin has blinded us to the truth.

Jesus came in contact with people just like us. And to those who were willing to acknowledge their blindness, He gave sight. But those who refused to let Him guide them He left in their blindness.

Do you want to see? You may not even know you have any blind spots, yet all of us do. So before you go any further, enter into God's presence through prayer, asking the Holy Spirit to work on your spiritual eyes as you work through this session of our study. Then, when He shows you the truth about yourself, don't close your eyes to it. Instead, ask Him to give you strength to look at it for what it is and to depend on Him to help you deal with it honestly and honorably. That's a request He is delighted to answer.

Read Proverbs 20:12; Matthew 13:13–16; 1 Corinthians 1:19; Ephesians 4:17–24.

Questions:

What does it mean to have spiritual eyes?

_____

_____

When have you seen another totally unaware of an area of spiritual blindness in his or her life?

_____

_____

In what areas of your own life do you find it difficult to believe the truth and accept Jesus' answer?

_____

_____

What inhibits your willingness to face these areas of blindness and allow the Lord to deal with them?

_____

_____

Behind the Scenes

Jesus' disciples questioned Him about the reason for a certain man's blindness. They believed his blindness was a result of sin, and they were not alone in their belief about the cause of physical handicaps. Some Jewish texts of that day taught that the soul of a person could sin in a preexistent state. Many believed that a baby still in the womb could have feelings, even sinful ones. And it was widely held that Exodus 20:5 and 34:6–7 taught that one's descendants would be punished for one's sins. The disciples wanted Jesus to resolve this theological issue for them in regard to this blind man.

Jesus' answer to His disciples didn't resolve their theological inquiry. In fact, it didn't say at all what caused this man's blindness. All says is what can be done through it.

Beyond the tragedy of human defects, which result in a general way from man's fall and the consequent entry of sin, sickness, affliction, and death into the world, God's merciful and sovereign grace is available.

Word Wealth—*Works*

Works: Greek *ergon* (er'-gon); Strong's *#2041*: Toil, occupation, enterprise, deed, task, accomplishment, employment, performance, work, labor, course of action. The miraculous accomplishments and deeds of Jesus are works of God implying power and might. Compare "energy" and "urge."

Kingdom Extra

Read 1 Kings 17:17–24. Often we do not understand the reason for sickness. The widow of Zarephath questioned Elijah's responsibility (1 Kings 17:18); Elijah questioned God's reasonableness (v. 20); then, lying prostrate on the child, he cried out in intercession to the Lord (v. 21)—and resurrection was the result. Healing comes as we move from reasoning over questions of *why* and begin responding to *how* the Lord works through faith-filled prayer. The Lord desires to heal.

Read Matthew 8:2–3.

Questions:

Have you ever prayed for healing that didn't occur?

What are the possible reasons for this? Support your answer biblically.

✎ _____

_____

Blind Guides

The healing of this blind man (John 9:1–41) caused great consternation for the Pharisees—the reigning legalists of the day—and prompted an investigation and interrogation. Their perverse reasoning placed them in a dilemma from which the only escape was to disprove the miracle that had been preformed. They argued that no miracle could have occurred because it was the Sabbath, and God would never violate the law of rest by healing a person. However, the fact that a man born blind now had perfect sight refuted their theory. Thus, they must either deny the facts or confess the divine nature of Jesus. The logic of the healed man was simple and irrefutable (vv. 30–33). Unable to deny the man's testimony, the religious authorities took the cowardly way out and excommunicated him.

Read 2 Timothy 3:1–7.

Questions:

According to this passage, what are the sinful attitudes that impede recognition of truth?

✎ _____

_____

Which of these exist in your own heart?

✎ _____

_____

What steps can you take to be freed of these sinful attitudes?

✎ _____

_____

 Kingdom Life—Use Spiritual Eyes

When some of the Pharisees overheard Jesus' words, they asked Him somewhat arrogantly if He was suggesting that they were blind to the truth (John 9:40). After all, they were the strict teachers of the law. If anyone knew the truth, they did. Jesus' reply is penetrating (v. 41) but at first blush, enigmatic. Jesus moved the discussion from physical blindness to spiritual blindness. To believe in Jesus means to see spiritually, whereas those who do not believe in Him remain blind, caught in the darkness of their own sin.

Remember that God's judgment is a boon of *deliverance* to those who trust Him, but a curse upon those who resist Him. Judgment, as in a lawsuit's resolution, works both ways.

Read John 8:31–36; Romans 6:14–18; 8:1–4.

Questions:

How does sin create areas of darkness in our lives?

_____

_____

What are the areas of darkness in your own life?

_____

_____

What is the freedom we are given through Christ?

_____

_____

How does this freedom enable us to see?

_____

_____

Probing the Depths

We often hear John 10:10 quoted, but do we really understand its meaning? God's covenant to us is a covenant for abundant life. From the very beginning of time, Scripture shows us that God wanted us to be happy and prosperous. In Genesis we are told that God made everything and declared it to be good. Then He gave this beautiful, plentiful earth to Adam; Adam was given dominion over all of it (Genesis 1:28). God's plan from the beginning was for man to be enriched and to have a prosperous, abundant life. Here Jesus declares His intention to recover and restore to man what was the Father's intent and to break and block the Devil's intent to hinder our receiving it.

Read Ephesians 3:20–21.

Questions:

Do you experience abundant life?

✎_____

_____

Why do you believe this is so?

✎_____

_____

What spiritual changes need to happen within you in order for you to walk in the abundant life Jesus promises?

✎_____

_____

Word Wealth—*Abundantly*

Abundantly: Greek *perissos* (per-is-sos'); Strong's #*4053*: Superabundance, excessive, overflowing, surplus, over and above, more than enough, profuse, extraordinary, above the ordinary, more than sufficient.

Kingdom Life—*We Are Sheep, He Is the Shepherd*

Jesus' third "I am" pronouncement depicts Him as "the door of the sheep" (John 10:7). This imagery contrasts Jesus' protection of the sheep in the fold with the usurpers, the false prophets of Old Testament times and the false messiahs of more recent times. Entering the sheepfold through Jesus is a saving action and provides the sheep with abundant life and provision.

The phrase in John 10:9, "go in and out," does not mean that one can vacillate about being in Christ one moment and outside of Him the next. The picture is one of security and safety in Christ as the door to the daily comings and goings of the sheep.

"I am the good shepherd" (v. 11). In this fourth pronouncement, Jesus declares Himself to be the owner of the sheep. He contrasts His genuine concern for His sheep with the conduct of a hireling, whose only interest is in self-preservation.

The Pharisees would have been very familiar with the shepherding illustration. This imagery is used throughout the Old Testament.

Read Genesis 49:24; Psalms 23:1; 80:1; Isaiah 40:10–11; 56:9–12; Jeremiah 23:1–4; 25:32–38; Ezekiel 34.

Questions:

What insight do these passages give regarding Jesus as "the door of the sheep" (John 10:7) and the "good shepherd" (v. 11)?

In what ways have you experienced Jesus' shepherding heart?

Kingdom Life—*You Are Gods*

In John 10:34, Jesus quotes Psalms 82:6: "You are gods." Jesus does not speak here of false gods, nor does He deify humanity. Rather He confers a title of commendation, noting the God-given capacities of human life and will, the fruit of being made in His image.

Jesus argues that since the Scriptures cannot be broken—nullified or made void—and they refer to certain people as gods, then there should be no perceived problem with His referring to Himself as the Son of God, especially in view of His special relationship to the Father.

He's willing to rest His entire case for His unity with the Father on the fact that His miraculous works verify that unity (John 10:37–38). In other words if His claim to unity is false, how could His ability to cure congenital blindness with spit and clay or to make lame men walk or to turn water into wine be accounted for? Such acts are supernatural and find their source only in God.

Read Psalm 82.

Questions:

In what ways are God's words here applicable to each of His children?

✎ _____

_____

_____

Which stand out most to you and why?

✎ _____

_____

_____

 Word Wealth—*Sanctified*

Sanctified: Greek *hagiazo* (hag-ee-ad'-zo); Strong's #37: To hallow, set apart, dedicate consecrate, separate, sanctify, make holy. *Hagiazo* as a state of holiness is the opposite of *koinon,* meaning common or unclean. In the Old Testament, things, places, and ceremonies were named *hagiazo.* In the New Testament the word describes a manifestation of life produced by the indwelling Holy Spirit. Because His Father set Him apart, Jesus is appropriately called the Holy One and rightly proclaims Himself "sanctified" (John 10:36).

Record Your Thoughts

How about you? Is your faith based on keeping certain religious formulas, traditions, or practices, on pleasing certain people, obeying certain moral codes, or on any other thing or duty? If confidence and convictions are not rooted in the triune God—Father, Son, and Holy Spirit—if anyone thinks to reach heaven or perfection or spiritual maturity through any other avenue, then they are dead wrong. Belief begins and is sustained forever in the Lord alone. No one else is sufficient. Is there any area of your life where this absolute dependence on Him needs to be asserted? Make sure you settle this matter with Him today.

Realities of Life

John 10:40—12:50

Kingdom Key—*Know the Mind of Christ*

Isaiah 55:8–9 "My thoughts are not your thoughts, nor are your ways My ways," says the LORD. "For as the heavens are higher than the earth, so are My ways higher than your ways, and My thoughts than your thoughts."

Obviously, our thinking must change if we are to understand the kingdom. God's kingdom operates in a much different way than the world in which we live. Jesus taught us the ways of the kingdom and often His words seem contradictory: to gain you must lose, to rule you must serve, to live you must die. However, these statements make perfect sense when you explore the depths of their meaning. Jesus proved them true in His own life.

Jesus gave up His heavenly glory in order to regain it and enlarge it with the glorification of spiritual children such as you and me. As the ruler over all, He became the model servant to all. And He understood that by committing Himself to serve the Father in life, He would have to die.

Jesus faced and worked through the hard realities of life. But He was not stoic about them. They impacted Him; they stirred up His feelings, His compassion, His anger, His love. We'll see this fact about Him very clearly in John 11 and 12. We'll see Him bring life out of death, but not before it evokes His tears and anger. We'll also see Him heralded as the king of Israel while He prepares to die at the hands of the Jewish leaders. And, if we'll look closely, we'll see in Him how we can deal with life's paradoxes and come out on top, even when it appears that the world has us down for good.

Read 1 Corinthians 2:16.

Questions:

What does it mean to have the mind of Christ?

_____

_____

What other examples of paradox can you locate in Scripture?

_____

_____

Why do you believe paradox exists in kingdom principles?

_____

_____

 Kingdom Extra

Paradoxes, as used in Scripture, are pregnant with meaning, but they can truly challenge our minds. They present us with truths that appear to have no way of being true and are totally alien to our experience. Paradoxes seem to contradict themselves. One wonders why God would choose to communicate in such a seemingly complicated way.

We know that God exists in the spiritual realm, a dimension beyond the physical world. To attempt to impose the limits, restrictions, and expectations of our world on the spiritual realm is senseless. It is a place and a state of being that is simply "other." It is a place of the eternal, a concept beyond our limited intellect.

When God communicates eternal truth to us, our language and earthbound minds limit our ability to receive the message. By speaking in ways that seem contradictory to our experience, God challenges us to reach beyond our limited understanding and enter into that spiritual realm.

As we ponder and explore the paradoxes of Scripture, we inevitably discover that they are true, that they provide insight into reality we have never seen before. Consequently, they tend to transform our perspective, and in so doing, they usually change our motivations and the way we behave.

Read Luke 22:24–30; Ephesians 5:22–33; 6:5–9; Matthew 6:19–21; Luke 12:13–34; 1 Timothy 6:17–19.

Question:

What are some ways the paradoxes in Scripture have proven true in your own life?

✎_____

_____

 Kingdom Life—*Trust God's Timing*

God's timetable is rarely in accord with ours because He usually wants to do something greater in our circumstances than we could ever imagine.

Jesus could have gone to Bethany and healed Lazarus while he was still sick. Instead, He delayed for two days. Jesus' delay underscored what He had taught consistently: that His marching orders came exclusively from His Father. Neither the need of His closest friends nor the fury of His enemies determined His actions. The Father had a plan in mind. He wanted to show through His Son that He had authority over death, not just disease. And by doing so, both the Father and the Son would be glorified.

The story of Lazarus being raised from death is a prime example of divine sovereignty amid human suffering.

Read Isaiah 55:8–9; Proverbs 3:5–6.

Questions:

In what way have you experienced a delay in receiving an answer to prayer?

✎_____

_____

_____

Have you ever received an answer that was completely different than what you expected?

✎_____

_____

_____

In what ways were God's timing and His answer better than what you asked/expected?

_____

_____

_____

_____

Behind the Scenes

Martha's belief that Lazarus would "rise again in the resurrection at the last day" (John 11:24) was very common in first-century Judaism. Almost all in the Jewish world (the exception being the Sadducees: Matthew 22:23; Mark 12:18) accepted the idea that at the end of the world, all humankind would be resurrected from the dead, unbelievers to divine condemnation and believers to divine blessing (Psalms 16:8–11; 73:23–26; Isaiah 26:14; Daniel 12:1–4). But the idea that the resurrection of an isolated individual could occur in history, before the world ended, was totally foreign to them. Consequently, Martha's confession in Jesus as the divine Messiah does not mean that she believed He would raise Lazarus before the end of the age. What Jesus eventually did surprised even her.

Kingdom Life—*Resurrection and Life*

Jesus' fifth "I am" statement is found in John 11:25: "I am the resurrection and the life. He who believes in Me, though he may die, he shall live."

Martha knew the Old Testament and so she believed in a resurrection. But she didn't believe Jesus could help in the present situation. Lazarus was dead.

So often we can believe the Lord for our tomorrows, but today we accept despair. Jesus is the "resurrection and the life" today. Life begins at the moment a person accepts the Savior. All the old passes away, and we are born again into a new life, an abundant life. We die to our old lives and are resurrected into God's kingdom. (This reality is recognized in the physical form of baptism by immersion.) Resurrection power is a present power, working in the lives of all those who know Jesus as Savior and Lord.

Read Romans 6:1–14.

Questions:

What benefits do we receive through entering into Christ's death and resurrection?

✎_____

_____

How do you experience the reality of resurrection life in your daily walk?

✎_____

_____

 Kingdom Life—*Emotions: Neither Right nor Wrong*

Whether you are a man or a woman, you may have trouble expressing your emotions. Perhaps you're afraid of what others might think, or maybe you grew up in a home where emotions couldn't be expressed, only stifled. It may be that you fear that negative emotions are sinful (anger, sorrow, frustration). Whatever the reason, know that Jesus saw nothing wrong with letting deep feelings flow from His being for all to see.

Jesus wept when He saw the sorrow in His friends. He felt the sorrow and shed compassionate tears. His deep emotion caused Him to groan within Himself. The word translated as "groaning" expresses anger, deeply rooted emotion, and stern admonishment. Jesus' emotional response was strong and expressed in His actions and demeanor.

It is not the emotion that is either right or wrong. It is the heart attitude that produces the emotion that we must be concerned with. A heart filled with sinful motivation can engender emotional responses that are not in keeping with kingdom principles. Even then, we can bring "every thought into captivity" (2 Corinthians 10:5) and refuse to act upon sinful impulses. It is also true that God may use our emotions to prompt us to godly purposes.

We must listen to our emotions, for they reveal much about our relationship to the world around us. The emotion itself is not right or wrong; it is our reasons and responses that must be considered.

Read Proverbs 4:23; 12:25; Matthew 12:33–37; 2 Corinthians 10:5.

Questions:

What other examples of Jesus' emotional responses can you locate in Scripture?

✎_____

_____

_____

What emotions do you have trouble expressing?

✎_____

_____

Why do you believe this is so?

✎_____

_____

_____

Can you think of a time when negative emotions have caused you to respond in ways that were detrimental or sinful?

✎_____

_____

How can our responses to negative emotions actually promote life for ourselves and others?

✎_____

_____

Behind the Scenes

The council that convened to discuss Jesus (John 11:47) was the Sanhedrin. Caiaphas, who was the son-in-law of Annas (John 18:13), was the high priest who headed the Sanhedrin from A.D. 18 to A.D. 36. A Sadducee, he saw Jesus as a threat to Judea. If the people tried to make Jesus the Messiah-King, Rome would come down on the nation and destroy it, so Caiaphas urged political expediency—sacrifice Jesus for the preservation of the nation. Unknowingly, however, Caiaphas's choice of action was prophetic. Jesus' death would indeed be good for the nation, not for its physical preservation, but rather for its spiritual salvation.

Kingdom Extra

Spikenard (John 12:3) is a valuable and fragrant ointment derived from the dried roots of the herbal plant called nard. By the first century A.D. it was already being imported from its native India in alabaster boxes. Because of its costliness, spikenard was used only for very special occasions.

Judas complained at the extravagance of Mary's devotion (v. 5). The spikenard she used to anoint Jesus was worth a year's wages. Judas's feigned concern for the poor is contrasted with Mary's desire to serve Jesus. He was more important to her than any possession or any other person. She knew who He was, and she gave Him the best that she had.

Read 2 Samuel 24:24; 1 Chronicles 21:24.

Questions:

What is at the heart of David's refusal to offer to the Lord "that which costs me nothing" (2 Samuel 24:24; 1 Chronicles 21:24)?

✎_____

_____

In what ways do you fail to give only your best to the Lord?

✎_____

_____

Behind the Scenes

Due to the signs Jesus had performed, especially the raising of Lazarus from the dead, the people were ecstatic to see Jesus coming to the Passover. Many had come to believe that He was the expected Messiah, but the Messiah they were looking for was a political one—a mighty Warrior-King who would lead them in battle against their enemies, achieving victory and reestablishing the independence of their nation. Their laying palm branches in the road before Jesus was a symbol of their nationalism and sense of impending victory. And their shouting "Hosanna" (which means "please save" or "save now"), and calling Him the Coming One and the King of Israel, served only to reiterate their belief that He was entering the city as their political Savior.

Kingdom Life—*See Him*

Jesus' words in John 12:23–50 are the last words He addressed to the public (other than at His trial). There is a sense of finality, a last appeal.

Certain Greeks who had come to the Passover Feast asked the disciples if they could see Jesus. When the disciples approached Jesus with the men's request, He spoke of losing life in order to gain it and gave the invitation to follow Him and serve Him.

He redefined His impending death. The sufferings of Jesus, and particularly His death, were the Father's profoundest occasion to glorify Him. Jesus was not glorified in His resurrection and ascension as much as in His sacrificial death on the cross. The cross is at the heart of the church's mission and message. The cross dethroned Satan's uncontested rulership in the world. The cross is the sole hope and means for full reinstatement to relationship with God and rulership under Him—to reign in life (Romans 5:17).

Finally, He speaks of His purpose and mission. He came to be a light in the world, enabling any who believe to see the Father through Him. His final statement is His assurance that all He has spoken has been by command of the Father.

Read Isaiah 6:9–10; Matthew 10:39; 16:24–25; John 8:26–29; Galatians 6:14; Philippians 2:5–11; 3:7–11; Colossians 2:14–15.

Questions:

With these Scripture portions in mind, how do we see Jesus?

_____

_____

What is the result in our lives?

_____

_____

Word Wealth—*Darkness*

Darkness: Greek *scotia* (skot-ee'-ah); Strong's #4653: Darkness, gloom, evil, sin, obscurity, night, ignorance, moral depravity. The New Testament especially uses the word in a metaphorical sense of ignorance of divine truth, man's sinful nature, total absence of light, and a lack of spiritual perception. Light equals happiness. *Scotia* equals unhappiness. *Scotia* as spiritual darkness basically describes everything earthly or demonic that is at enmity with God.

Record Your Thoughts

Questions:

In what ways has this session brought you to a fuller understanding of the mind of Christ?

✎ _____

_____

_____

What truth encountered here has most impacted you and why?

✎ _____

_____

_____

What can you learn from Jesus' example about how to handle stubborn unbelief, mistaken notions about Christianity, and even cowardly belief?

✎ _____

_____

_____

SESSION TEN

Servant Power

John 13:1—14:14

 Kingdom Key—*We Are Empowered to Serve*

Acts 1:8 You shall receive power when the Holy Spirit has come upon you; and you shall be witnesses to Me in Jerusalem, and in all Judea and Samaria, and to the end of the earth.

People with power usually love their power; they're infatuated with their influence over people and situations, whatever it is they strive to control.

Jesus was a powerful person. Anyone who could create a universe out of nothing, sustain it by His word, and alter it at will has power beyond our wildest dreams. Of course, those activities belong to His deity. What about His humanity? How did He show and exercise power as a man? The answer is fascinating.

Jesus subjugated His power to the Father. His submission was so thorough that everything He did, He did with the Father's prior direction and permission. He would not heal a paralytic or a blind man, turn water into wine, raise a man from the dead, tell the people that He was one with the Father (even if that would enrage them), unless specifically directed by the Father. (Note John 5:19, 30; 7:16; 8:28–29 as examples.)

This is the most potent power in the world: *servant power.* It can never be misused because it always obeys God. It will always accomplish what it's intended to because God will back it all the way. It will do only good, because the all-good God is its source, sustainer, guide, and goal. It can never be tyrannical, because its source is God; and He is always motivated by perfect love, because that's exactly what He is. It can never be defeated, because nothing in the universe can effectively compete with its all-powerful source. And Jesus had this power as no one has before or since. He was the Servant par excellence; He has no equal.

How can we tap into the power Jesus had? There's only one way: Jesus' way, which is the Father's way. Let's discover what John has to say about the Helper who is necessary to make servant power an effective reality in our daily lives.

Read Matthew 7:21–23; Acts 2:17; Romans 8:26–27; 12:1; 1 Corinthians 2:10–16; 6:19–20; Philippians 2:1–11; Ephesians 3:14–21; 6:5–8; 1 Peter 4:10–11.

Questions:

What does servant power look like in action?

_____

_____

What role does the Holy Spirit play in your day-to-day life?

_____

_____

Are your life, your ministry, and your will subjugated to the Father? Explain your answer.

_____

_____

Do you continually seek God's will in situations and choices? Explain your answer.

_____

_____

What do you believe is the message of Matthew 7:21–23 regarding servant power?

_____

_____

Kingdom Life—*Start with the Basics*

Jesus knew the Father's will. All through the gospel we see indications of that. If we are to walk in the servant power of Jesus, we must also know the Father's will. We learn that through His written Word, by seeking the counsel of godly men and women, and, most important, by listening to His voice within. We cannot understand His written Word without His revelation, we cannot glean truth from others without His confirmation, and we cannot hear His voice unless we listen.

Prayer is the vehicle through which we become attuned to the voice of God. True prayer is founded upon finding and coming into agreement with God's will. We ask according to His will; then we stand in faith, confident that God hears us and that what we ask for is already ours. To pray with authority and receive answers to your prayers, make sure you ask according to the will of God. If you do not know His will, ask Him. Then believe that He hears your petition and has already set the answer in motion. Pray tenaciously and persistently until His will is accomplished. That is true prayer and the only way to servant power.

Read 1 John 5:14; James 1:5.

Questions:

When do you find it difficult to hear the voice of God?

_____

_____

What steps can you take to improve your ability to discern His voice?

_____

_____

How can hearing the voice of God cause a greater ability to experience signs and wonders in your own life and ministry?

_____

_____

Word Wealth—*Humility*

Humility: Greek *tapeinophrosune* (tap-eye-nof-ros-oo'-nay); Strong's #5012: Modesty, lowliness, humble-mindedness, a sense of moral insignificance, and a humble attitude of unselfish concern for the welfare of others. It is a total absence of arrogance, conceit, and haughtiness. The word is a combination of *tapeinos,* "humble," and *phren,* "mind." The word was unknown in classical nonbiblical Greek. Only by abstaining from self-aggrandizement can members of the Christian community maintain unity and harmony.

Kingdom Life—*Humble Yourself*

If pride is the greatest sin—and it is—then humility must be the greatest virtue. It is humility that allows us to acknowledge that God has a claim on our lives, that we are fallible, mortal creatures, and that God is the Master of the universe. It is humility that says, "I am a sinner, and I need to be saved." The truths of the kingdom are perceived only by those who are humble. No one who is proud will ever gain anything from God. Those who are humble receive the grace of God and are given the secrets of the kingdom, because they come as beggars. Jesus Christ said, "Blessed are the poor in spirit, for theirs is the kingdom of heaven" (Matthew 5:3).

Jesus showed forth this type of humility when He washed the disciples' feet. Usually, a servant performed the menial task of washing the guests' feet. Jesus assumed that role. He used this occasion to teach a lesson in humility and selfless service.

Read Proverbs 22:4; James 4:6.

Questions:

Why is humility the beginning of wisdom?

_____

_____

What does it mean that "God resists the proud" (James 4:6)?

_____

_____

How can we possess the kingdom of heaven now?

_____

_____

In what ways do you put self aside and serve others for Christ's sake?

_____

_____

In what ways does pride rule in your life?

_____

_____

Kingdom Life—*Have Courage*

Read John 13:18–30. This is one of the most tragic sections of Scripture. Put yourself in Christ's sandals. He spent more than three years building into the lives of the twelve disciples, knowing that a time would come when one of the Twelve would violate His trust and spit on His teaching and turn Him over to His enemies. Yet, He told Judas, "What you do, do quickly" (v. 27). Those words took incredible courage. Without hedging or backing down, He set the wheels of His own betrayal in motion. Why? So the Father's will would be fulfilled, and through it His disciples would come to a firmer belief in Him as the predicted messianic God-man.

Can you serve with that kind of courage? Are you willing to sacrifice all—your time, energy, plans, hopes, dreams, finances, possessions, relationships, even your life—for the Lord and His work, if He so chooses? Would you even permit yourself to be betrayed for the sake of the kingdom? Pour out to God your fears, concerns, everything standing in your way of serving Him with selfless boldness and determination. Let Him work in your heart to increase your courage for Him.

Read Psalm 27:14; 31:23–24; Isaiah 35:3–10; 41:10; 43:1–5; Matthew 10:29–31.

Questions:

What lies at the heart of courage in the kingdom?

_____

_____

How might these qualities be strengthened in your life?

_____

_____

In what ways does fear impede your ability to walk effectively in the kingdom?

_____

_____

What steps can you take to decrease the effects of fear in your life?

Kingdom Life—*Express Love*

Though words may speak love, love is not contained in words. Feelings may accompany love, but love is not dependent on feelings. The love Jesus has for us and commands us to have for one another is *agape* love. This love is sacrificial, unconditional, constant, self-sustaining, and always seeking the best for and of the other person.

As you work through the questions below, do not allow guilt to overcome you. This exercise is meant to show you how great servant love really is. Just be honest before the Lord so He can better work in your life and bring *agape* love alive in your life.

Read 1 Corinthians 13:4–8.

Question:

Taking each characteristic listed in this Scripture portion separately, how does your love compare to the love described in 1 Corinthians 13:4–8?

Kingdom Extra

Christ's new commandment in John 13:34 presses us beyond our natural human inclinations to the need for Christ's inspiration. Christ's love for us is not dependent on a quality in us that makes us lovable. He loves us regardless of our strengths or weaknesses. That thought may be humbling to some who want to be chosen, called, and cherished because of their human credentials of talent, personality, or achievement. Christ's love is not motivated by any of these human qualities, but it is grace-motivated. If we are to love in His way, we will have to take seriously that we must ask for the ability and be empowered by the Holy Spirit. (See John 14:14, 16.)

Kingdom Life—*He Is the Way, the Truth, and the Life*

Although Jesus' disciples had been with Him, seeing His miracles, hearing His teaching, receiving private lessons in theology and life, and observing firsthand the outworking of His compassion and convictions, they still didn't completely understand as they would need to. So, once again, Jesus went over who He was and what He had come to do.

In His sixth "I am" statement, Jesus is threefold. He is the "way" (John 14:6) to the Father. There is no other. In order to enter through this way He has opened, we must realize He is the Word of God, the living truth of God embodied. Jesus is God, and as such, the very life of God.

Belief in Christ as God is the fundamental of fundamentals. If that is false, so is Christianity. Jesus provides the only way for us to know the Father, for He died in our place, freeing us from the penalty of sin. He reveals the truth to us and provides us with everlasting, abundant life. If the truth of Jesus' identity and purpose is not a settled fact in your heart and mind, servant power will always remain elusive to you.

Probing the Depths

We often hear of Jesus' promise that we will do "greater works than" those Jesus performed (John 14:12). This promise is not that His disciples will perform works that are greater in value or significance than His; rather, they will be greater in scope and number.

A vital key to walking in the pathway of God's miracles is to stay available to the implications of Jesus' words. When blessing comes in your work, service, or ministry, it is tempting to accept that this is all God has for you. It might be easy to stop and rest rather than keep your hand to the plow (Luke 9:62). Instead, refuse to allow the blessings of God's grace on your work to lead you to think that He may not be ready to do even more in your life. He does not call you to attempt to produce more, but to ask and believe Him for more, for the greater works He has in store for us to receive and, by His grace, achieve for His kingdom's purposes and glory. Keep your heart set and ready for the next advance for His kingdom.

Jesus will help us do greater works than He did by manifesting

His changeless mightiness through answered prayer. That's our assurance. He promised that He would not leave us to our own resources. We can draw upon His, and they are unlimited.

 Kingdom Extra

After assessing yourself against the basics, do you feel inadequate to the task? Does it seem that you could never meet the basic requirements, so servant power could never be a part of your experience? If you answered yes, you're not only being honest, you're absolutely correct. These basics are beyond the reach of all of us, if we try to attain them in our own power. You see, servant power is really a gift, not an acquisition. And there's only one way to receive it: through Christ. We must first believe that He is the Son of God, the Savior of the world, our Deliverer, and we must put our trust in Him. Then, and only then, Jesus supplies the rest of what we need: the One He called the Helper. This One is the Holy Spirit, the third person of the blessed Trinity. He empowers us to live as servants; without Him, our attempts at servanthood would be poor imitations of the real thing. He is the final key, the power key, and we'll learn more about Him in the next session.

So don't despair. God never gives us a command to do something without also giving us the ability to obey it. And in this case, our ability is wrapped up in the omnipotence of the Holy Spirit.

Record Your Thoughts

Questions:

Make a list of areas where you would like to begin to see "greater works" (John 14:12) accomplished by the Holy Spirit's power.

✎_____

_____

In light of this session's content, what areas of your life are hindering your ability to experience the greater works?

✎_____

_____

If you haven't already, how about committing here, today, to making prayer a daily affair? Seek the Lord. Discern His will. Then pray for the accomplishing of His purposes. After that, watch Him say, "Yes!" as your prayers release greater works according to His Word.

SESSION ELEVEN

The Divine Helper
John 14:15—16:33

 Kingdom Key—*Receive the Helper*

Acts 2:38–39 Repent, and let every one of you be baptized in the name of Jesus Christ for the remission of sins; and you shall receive the gift of the Holy Spirit. For the promise is to you and to your children, and to all who are afar off, as many as the Lord our God will call.

The Holy Spirit is the third person of the Trinity, the One who exercises the power of the Father and the Son in creation and redemption. Because the Holy Spirit is the source of the power by which believers come to Christ and see with new eyes of faith, He is closer than any words, short of *within us,* can describe, yet He focuses on One other than Himself. He is seldom in focus to be seen directly because He rather shows us Christ, the One through whom all life is to be seen in its new light.

The Holy Spirit appears in the gospel of John as the power by which Christians are brought to faith and helped to understand their walk with God. The Holy Spirit is the Paraclete, or Helper, whom Jesus promised to the disciples after His ascension. It is through the Helper that Father and Son abide with us.

Read Ezekiel 36:27; Luke 11:13; Acts 1:4–8; Romans 14:17; 15:13; 1 Corinthians 2:9–16; 6:19–20; Ephesians 1:13–14; 2 Timothy 1:13–14; Titus 3:4–7; 1 John 5:6–7.

Questions:

How have you experienced the working of the Paraclete in your own life?

In what ways have you failed to recognize the deity of the Holy Spirit?

_____

_____

In calling the Holy Spirit "another Helper" (John 14:16), what insight did Jesus give us into the Holy Spirit's role in our lives?

_____

_____

In what ways would a fuller recognition of the Holy Spirit's role in your life enable you to walk more effectively in the kingdom?

_____

_____

Note: We're going to move through this section of Scripture a bit differently. Rather than taking the verses in order, we're going to approach them topically. This will help us experience a more systematic approach to their teaching.

Word Wealth—*Another Helper*

Another: Greek *allos* (al'-los); Strong's *#243*: One besides another of the same kind. The word shows similarities but diversities of operation and ministries. Jesus' use of *allos* for sending another Helper equals "one besides Me and in addition to Me, but one just like Me. He will do in My absence what I would do if I were physically present with you." The Spirit's coming assures continuity with what Jesus did and taught.

Helper: Greek *parakletos* (par-ak'-lay-tos); Strong's *#3875*: From *para,* meaning "beside," and *kaleo,* meaning "to call." Literally, *parakletos* means "to call to one's side." The word signifies an intercessor, comforter, helper, advocate, counselor. In nonbiblical literature *parakletos* had the technical meaning of an attorney who appears in court in another's behalf. The Holy Spirit leads believers to a greater apprehension of gospel truth.

Probing the Depths

It is important that we realize the role of the Holy Spirit in our lives. Read closely John 14:16–26; 15:26; and 16:5–15. These passages reveal a great deal about the

Holy Spirit: His nature, His work, His relationship to the Father and Son, His relationship to believers and nonbelievers, the timing of His arrival, and how He can be known and received.

In the area below, record your discoveries. In the right-hand column, record any comments you would like to make: questions, observations, points of application. The object is to interact with the text, to let it speak to you and to respond back. Remember, God's Word is living and active, not dead and impotent (Hebrews 4:12), so give it an opportunity to enter into dialogue with you. The conversation will only help you.

	MY DISCOVERIES	**MY COMMENTS**
14:16–18		
14:15, 26		
15:26		
16:5–15		

Behind the Scenes

In John 14:17 Jesus tells us that the Holy Spirit dwells with and in us. This distinction points out the difference in the Holy Spirit's manner of work in the Old Testament and from pentecost on. During the old covenant the Holy Spirit was available to and present with some believers for selective purposes and only temporarily (Judges 3:10; 6:34; 11:29; 13:25; 1 Samuel 16:14; Psalm 51:11). Under the new covenant that Jesus ushered in through His death, resurrection, and ascension, the Spirit forever indwells all believers upon their initial confession of faith (Ezekiel 36:27; Romans 8:11; 1 Corinthians 6:19; 12:13). Then, through welcoming His overflowing fullness, believers receive the Spirit's power for ministry, service, obedience, and sanctification (Romans 8:4).

Kingdom Extra

Within this section of Scripture, there is much material for application. We will concentrate here on three key points that have great bearing on our daily walk. Let's take this opportunity for a Checkpoint in our walk of faith. Answer honestly. There is much to be gained by transparency before the Lord.

Checkpoint #1—Prayer

Jesus prayed—sincerely, faithfully, often. He is one with the Father, but in His humanity He depended upon prayer to let His requests be known. If the Son of man needed to pray, how much more do you? Prayer is essential to the Christian life. Share your thoughts about your prayer life. Note ways you can improve and grow in it.

✎ _____

_____

Checkpoint #2—Relationship with the Holy Spirit

The Holy Spirit was given to benefit us for the sake of Christ. We have looked closely at all the Holy Spirit was sent to bring into our lives. Without the Helper we cannot live consistently, faithfully, obediently, or powerfully. Share your thoughts about your relationship with the Holy Spirit. What role does He play in your life?

✎ _____

_____

Checkpoint #3—Response to Sin

The Holy Spirit convicts of sin. It is this conviction that leads us to the life-giving forgiveness found in our Lord. Conviction is not a feeling of guilt, but a heartfelt recognition of and sorrow for having disobeyed our Lord. Just as the Holy Spirit convicts us, He is the agent of conviction for the world.

When we live our lives without spending time with the Lord, our hearts can grow numb. Without the continual recognition of who we are and who He is, we tend to become cold and apathetic to the things of the Lord, and the conviction of the Holy Spirit becomes less and less discernible.

It is also true that we sometimes take upon ourselves the task of pointing out the areas of disobedience in the lives of others. That is *not* our job. We are sinners who should be telling other sinners where they can find forgiveness.

Share your thoughts about your response to sin in yourself and others. Be sure to go beyond thinking about your own heart condition and consider your current approach and attitudes in witnessing. Reflect on what you can do to improve both, leaving the Spirit to do His job while you do yours.

✎ _____

_____

 ## Kingdom Life—*Obedient Love*

Jesus completely aligned His life and will with the Father's (John 8:29), which indicates His total allegiance to the Father's Word and commandments. He also said He disapproved of any attitude that would reduce respect for or teach less than full obedience to the entirety of God's revealed Word. Thus, when He explicitly links His disciples' love for Him with their will to keep His commandments, we conclude Jesus' clear intent: if we love Him, we will love His Father's Word, also.

Read Matthew 5:17–19; 12:47–50.

Questions:

In what ways do you find obedience to God a difficult task?

✎ _____

_____

What does this say of your love for the Lord?

✎ _____

_____

What does Jesus mean when He equates doing the will of God with being His "brother and sister and mother" (Matthew 12:50)?

✎ _____

_____

Kingdom Life—*He Is the True Vine*

Jesus said, "I am the true vine" (John 15:1). This seventh "I am" statement is Jesus' last self-designation in the gospel of John. In it Jesus reveals to us that in order to experience growth, maturity, and productivity for the kingdom of God, we must abide in Him.

Jesus refers to God the Father here as the "vinedresser" (John 15:1). The fruit that the heavenly vinedresser looks for in His people is Christlikeness. In order to be productive, a branch must submit to pruning (the beneficent discipline of the Father) and must maintain an abiding union with the true vine.

When we abide in Christ, our prayers are effective, we glorify God in our fruit bearing, we demonstrate our discipleship, and our joy becomes full through experiencing Christ's own joy within us.

If you find yourself falling short of abundant fruitfulness, that's okay. Fruit bearing takes time; it's a process, one that God is committed to seeing you through. Your job is to abide in Christ, to stay by His side no matter what, seeking to obey Him through the empowerment of the Holy Spirit. The Spirit will handle the rest.

Read 1 John 2:24–29; 4:12–16.

Questions:

From this passage, how do you understand the term *abide*?

_____

_____

What signs exist in your own life that you abide in the vine (John 15:4)?

_____

_____

Behind the Scenes

The vine is one of the Old Testament images used to depict Israel (Psalm 80:8–16; Isaiah 5:1–7; Jeremiah 2:21; 5:10; 12:10; Ezekiel 15:1–8; 17:1–10; Hosea 10:1). When Jesus uses this imagery in John's gospel, it is to identify Himself as the true Israel, the One who fulfills what the nation of Israel failed to do.

Kingdom Life—*Know Complete Joy*

Jesus points the way to joy, a divine quality of character that is possessed and given only by God. It is rooted in relationship with the Holy Spirit, not in earthly or material things. We receive a clearer, if more difficult, description of joy in Hebrews 12:2: "Looking unto Jesus . . . who for the joy that was set before Him endured the cross." Joy is derived from the confidence that the price of dying to our will holds the inevitable certainty of eventually realizing the triumph. For Jesus, bringing sons and daughters into fellowship with the Father was His delight, though the cross was the means to that eventual joy.

Read Psalms 16:11; 27:6; 43:4–5; Romans 15:13; Galatians 5:22; James 1:2–4.

Questions:

Do you experience the joy of the Lord in your daily walk?

_____

_____

In what way has your view of joy changed in considering these passages?

_____

_____

What now is your definition of true joy?

_____

_____

Kingdom Life—*You Will Suffer*

Jesus never told us that the Christian life would be free of pain or chaos; rather, He warned us that such would come because we identify ourselves with Him, the Light, and the world who has embraced the darkness cannot tolerate the Light, so the world fights against it, trying to snuff it out. Whether we like it or not, we are combatants, and the battle is unrelenting and brutal.

God's people will suffer persecution because of their devotion to Christ—that's indisputable. History bears out the truth of that statement, and if your experience hasn't proved it yet, it undoubtedly will if you are standing for Him, bearing fruit through His Spirit.

Read 1 Peter.

Questions:

In what ways have you suffered for your commitment to Christ?

_____

_____

What has been your reaction in the past?

_____

_____

How might the Lord call you to respond?

_____

_____

_____

In what other ways might we suffer for being the "light of the world" (Matthew 5:14)?

_____

_____

Kingdom Life—*Enabled to Minister*

The Holy Spirit draws from and conveys the authority of Christ. True ministry in the Holy Spirit never serves a private agenda. Rather, working in us and through us, He continually glorifies Christ, who glorifies the Father.

Jesus' life and character demonstrate how to minister to others as the Holy Spirit enables us. We are to minister in righteousness, truth, and power in order to witness to the world of our Lord and bring all to a saving relationship with our Lord.

Read 1 Corinthians 13:1–3; 1 John 3:14.

Questions:

What is to be at the root of our desire to minister to others?

✎_____

_____

What is your motivation for ministry?

✎_____

_____

In what ways is Christ's love evident in your ministry?

✎_____

_____

_____

In what ways do you fail to show forth the love of Christ in ministry?

✎_____

_____

_____

Kingdom Life—We Serve a Resurrected Lord

Jesus' resurrection is the most monumental and joyous event in all of biblical history. It demonstrates Christ's victory over sin, death, and Satan. When you add to that His ascension into heaven to rule with the Father's authority until all the power of His enemies has been vanquished, you realize that we are definitely on the winning side with Jesus, endowed with the promised power of His Spirit and with every reason to expect His victory day by day.

Record Your Thoughts

Questions:

What in this session struck you as most relevant to your situation?

✎_____

_____

_____

What changes has this session prompted you to make in your life and/or ministry?

✎ _____

_____

_____

How has this session changed your view of the Holy Spirit and His role in your life?

✎ _____

_____

_____

What one verse in this section stands out above all others for you? Why do you believe this is so?

✎ _____

_____

_____

SESSION TWELVE

To the Glory of God

John 17:1—21:25

 Kingdom Key—*Glorify God in All Things*

1 Corinthians 6:20 You were bought at a price; therefore glorify God in your body and in your spirit, which are God's.

Jesus' prayer found in John 17 might be more properly called "the Lord's Prayer." Though that is the name we attach to the Lord's example of right praying in Matthew 6:9–13, the words of John 17 record what the Lord prayed just before He was to die. It is a message sent from Jesus' heart to the Father's heart.

In this prayer Jesus voices His desire to glorify the Father. To glorify God is to make Him known. In all that Jesus was and did, He revealed the Father.

Believers in Jesus will know God. They, in turn, should show forth the glory of God. They should so live their lives as to reveal God to an unbelieving world.

Read Matthew 5:14–16; 2 Corinthians 1:19–22; Philippians 2:5–11.

Questions:

How does your life glorify God?

_____

_____

In what areas do you struggle to show forth the light you have been given?

_____

_____

What do you hope to gain through this study that will further enable you to glorify God by being a light to the world?

✎ _____

_____

Probing the Depths

Prayer is asking for needs and desires to be fulfilled. It is incredible to realize that Jesus—the Lord of all, Sustainer of all, Creator of all, Owner of all—asked. He placed Himself in the most humble position of a needy, dependent person, and He asked. In doing so He raised asking to a new level of dignity and sanctity. This simple, humble, commonplace activity is now special, even holy. Or at least it can be beyond what we could ever imagine.

Jesus' prayer recorded in John 17 is the prayer of a lifetime. It encapsulates not only what Jesus found to be most important but what we should as well. Our prayers can never go wrong if they follow Jesus' example. Jesus prays the Father's will. That's a sure guarantee that His prayer will be answered. If we want our requests to God answered, we must pray according to His will. So let's discover what that is. Jesus will show us, and His Spirit will impress it on our minds and hearts. Let those who have ears to hear, listen.

Read Matthew 6:5–8; 21:22; Mark 11:23–24; Luke 11:9.

Questions:

How can we know God's will prior to prayer?

✎ _____

_____

What promises do we have in regard to prayer?

✎ _____

_____

In what ways can you grow in your own prayer life?

✎ _____

_____

Have you ever experienced an unanswered prayer? Why do you believe this is so?

_____

_____

Kingdom Life—*Called to Unity*

Unity is Christ's miracle of oneness. In John 17 we hear His prayer for the same oneness for His disciples that He has with the Father. He and the Father share the same purpose, plan, and power. Christ often reminds us that He came not to do His own will, but to do the Father's will. Likewise, our unity is dependent on sharing the priority of seeking and doing the Lord's will. His desire for us is to reach those who do not know Him so that they, too, may become one with us and others who have accepted Him as Lord of their lives. The equation of oneness is profound, and yet, very simple: one plus one plus one equals one—Christ, ourselves, and another equals oneness. It is Christ in our brother or sister who reaches out to the Christ in us. We are united in and through Him. It is a miracle of the indwelling Christ.

Read Matthew 25:31–46; Romans 12:4; 1 Corinthians 12:12–27; Ephesians 4:11–16; Matthew 5:23–24.

Questions:

In what ways do you experience this oneness with other believers?

_____

_____

Why does our involvement in discord in the body of Christ hinder our ministry and ability to pray effectively?

_____

_____

In what ways can you more effectively walk in the unity Christ desires for you?

_____

_____

Kingdom Life—*Let Your Requests Be Known*

In this prayer in John 17, Jesus made six requests of His Father, and He joined each one with a reason, a purpose, or a goal. These requests reveal Jesus' desires and motivations. See if you can identify them as you look up the following verses.

	HIS REQUESTS	**HIS REASONS**
John 17:1–3, 5		
17:11		
17:15–16		
17:17–19		
17:20–21		
17:24		

Read John 15:24; Philippians 4:6; James 4:2–3.

Question:

What has been revealed to you about your own prayer life as you consider Jesus' prayer?

Word Wealth—*Glory/Glorify*

Glory: Greek *doxa* (dox'-ah); Strong's *#1391*: Originally, *doxa* conveyed the idea of an opinion or estimation in which one is held. Then the word came to denote the reputation, good standing, and esteem given to a person. It progressed to honor or recognition of transcendent attributes. In the New Testament, *doxa* becomes splendor, radiance, and majesty centered in Jesus. Here *doxa* is the majestic, absolute perfection residing in Christ and evidenced by the miracles He performed.

Glorify: Greek *doxadzo* (dox-ad'-zo); Strong's #*1392*: This verb conveys the idea of ascribing honor. It is to magnify, extol, or praise God for His majestic attributes. It is to speak forth in word, attitude, and deed the magnificence of the triune God.

 Kingdom Life—*Finish the Work*

Jesus' use of the word *glory* transcends the word's use as commonly expressed. In describing the glory of and His glorifying of God, Jesus means to make known (to make or leave a favorable impression or opinion of) the person and attributes of His Father. Jesus' earthly life clearly did that. He displayed on earth the splendor of a wondrously favorable impression of the Father. When humankind saw Jesus, they saw the Father.

But further, Jesus explains how He glorified God: He finished the work the Father gave Him to do. To glorify God, then, is to complete an assignment, to do those things He has called, chosen, appointed, and anointed us to do.

Read 1 Corinthians 10:31; Philippians 3:12–14; 1 Timothy 4:14–15; 2 Timothy 4:6–8.

Questions:

With this insight in mind (doing those things He has called, chosen, appointed, and anointed us to do), how does your life glorify God?

✎_____

_____

What part does obedience play in glorifying God?

✎_____

_____

 Kingdom Extra

Chapters 18–21 of John's gospel give his account of Jesus' betrayal, trials, death, burial, resurrection, postresurrection appearances, and His ascension. You may want

to compare John's account of these events with what the other gospel writers record. None of them provide a comprehensive account, so the comparisons can enrich your understanding of these pivotal, historical events.

Read Matthew 26:36—28:20; Mark 14:32—16:20; Luke 22:39—24:53.

 ## Kingdom Life—*Jesus Is God*

In the Garden of Gethsemane Judas fulfilled his betrayal of Jesus. He led an armed group of temple guards along with a contingent of priests and Pharisees to arrest Jesus. Jesus did not attempt to hinder their ghastly mission, but readily identified Himself by proclaiming, "I am He" (John 18:5).

On the surface these words seem a simple proclamation of Jesus' identity in terms of His name and hometown. However, at these words, "they drew back and fell to the ground" (John 18:6). The entire contingent was so overwhelmed by the power of Jesus' words that they could not stand in this momentary unleashing of His inherent power as God. So great was the impact that they seemingly were temporarily unmindful of their purpose.

Read Exodus 15:6–18; 1 Samuel 2:2–10; Isaiah 6:5.

Questions:

In what ways do you fail to remember Jesus' inherent power as God?

_____

_____

What responses can you find in Scripture to the manifest presence of God?

_____

_____

Are you continually aware of God's awesome presence in your life?

_____

_____

What would be the result of a life lived in constant recognition of God's power and love?

✎_____

_____

Kingdom Life—We Are Citizens of His Kingdom

John is the only gospel writer who records Jesus' words "My kingdom is not of this world" (John 18:36). At the time John wrote his gospel, Christians were often accused of the political desire to institute rulership of an earthly kingdom. But Jesus makes it clear in this statement that His rulership is not in conflict with any earthly government.

Jesus' kingdom is spiritual and eternal. We become citizens of that kingdom when we are born again and enter into its overriding commandments, statutes, laws, and purpose. When we become citizens of the eternal kingdom of God, we are given eternal life through Jesus.

But being a citizen of Jesus' kingdom has as much to do with quality of life as it does quantity. The idea of eternal life describes a divine dimension of life available to humankind, *now* as well as in the future.

Read Colossians 1:13–14; James 2:5; Revelation 2:10–11; Romans 8:14–39.

Questions:

The eternal is that which exists beyond space and time. Describe your view of the meaning of *eternal life.*

✎_____

_____

As a citizen of God's eternal kingdom, what should characterize your life?

✎_____

_____

What promises are yours as a result of your citizenship in God's kingdom?

✎_____

_____

Behind the Scenes

When Judea became a Roman imperial province in A.D. 6, Pontius Pilate was appointed by the emperor as the prefect, or governor, of the province. He served in this capacity until A.D. 36. Although his permanent residence was in Caesarea (Acts 23:23–24), Pilate stayed in Jerusalem during Jewish festival days so he was readily available to deal with crises and maintain order.

Ancient historians record that Pilate was a greedy, inflexible, and cruel leader hated by the Jews. In the case of Jesus, however, the Jewish authorities were willing to lay their hatred toward Pilate aside in order to exercise their greater hatred toward Jesus. You see, they could not carry out the death penalty under Roman law, but Pilate could. So they appealed to him to execute their vengeance.

When they brought Jesus to the Praetorium, the Roman governor's official residence, they wouldn't go inside "lest they should be defiled, but that they might eat the Passover" (John 18:28). Jewish tradition held that the dwellings of Gentiles were unclean, and so the Passover could not be observed by those who were ceremonially defiled. This verse poses a chronological problem. The other three gospels record that Jesus ate the Passover with His disciples on Thursday evening and was crucified the next day, Friday. John's gospel, however, says that the Jews had not eaten the Passover yet, even though it records earlier that Jesus and His disciples had already eaten the Passover lamb. What's going on?

Several solutions have been proposed, but the one that fits all the data the best is supplied by New Testament scholar Harold Hoehner. He presents evidence that suggests the Jews celebrated two Passovers during Jesus' time because of two different ways of reckoning the day. One way was to reckon a day from sunrise to sunrise, which was the method used by Jesus and the gospel writers, excluding John, and it was likely followed in Galilee. The other way was to determine a day from sunset to sunset, which seems to have been the official Jewish method followed by John and the Judeans. Therefore, if this hypothesis is right, Jesus and His disciples observed the Passover on Thursday with the Galileans, while the Judean Jews, which would have included the religious authorities in Jerusalem, sacrificed their Passover lambs Friday afternoon.

Kingdom Life—*He Died for You*

The account of Jesus' crucifixion is anything but pretty, but it is a record of what had to happen in order for Him to accomplish His mission for the Father and for us. So read it reverently; put yourself at the scene. See and touch the surroundings; hear and feel the anger, pain, and confusion. Don't let any detail pass by you. Remember, Jesus did this out of love—the purest, most precious love there could ever be. See if you can't understand it that way, and let the Holy Spirit do the rest.

Read Matthew 26:69—27:56; Mark 14:66—15:47; Luke 22:54—23:49.

Questions:

What new insights have you gained through your contemplation of Jesus' sacrifice on your behalf?

✎_____

_____

_____

How might this affect your day-to-day life?

✎_____

_____

_____

Behind the Scenes

Jesus died on the Passover. Three days later was Sunday, but not just any Sunday. The first Sunday after the Passover was the day when the Jews celebrated the Feast of Firstfruits. The firstfruits are the first ripened part of the harvest, furnishing actual evidence that the entire harvest is on the way. According to Leviticus 23:4–14, the firstfruits in connection with the Passover were used to consecrate the coming harvest.

Jesus' resurrection from death is what distinguishes Christianity from all other religions. It was a firstfruit—a promise of our own resurrection. In commemoration and celebration of this event, Christians gather on Sunday to worship the resurrected Lord.

Read Romans 8:18–30.

Questions:

What does it mean that we have the "firstfruits of the Spirit" (Romans 8:23)?

_____

_____

How is this made manifest in your own life?

_____

_____

Probing the Depths

Mary Magdalene remained outside the empty tomb alone, mourning Jesus' death and the disappearance of His body. When Christ appeared to her, He cautioned her, "Do not cling to Me" (John 20:17). His words reinforce the changed condition that now exists between Master and disciple. Jesus told Mary that this altered condition would be fully inaugurated at His ascension.

There is no justification for the carnal presumption asserted by sinful minds that some amorous feelings existed between Mary Magdalene and Jesus. Neither is there any evidence that Mary had been a prostitute, only that she had experienced a great deliverance (Luke 8:2).

Kingdom Life—*New Covenant Life*

Jesus appeared to His disciples on the very day of His resurrection. His first act was to breathe on them and say, "Receive the Holy Spirit" (John 20:22). The allusion to Genesis 2:7 is unmistakable. Now Jesus breathed life into His own.

Some interpret Jesus' words as symbolic and as anticipating pentecost. Others understand the Greek word *lambano* (lam-ban'-o), Strong's #2983, translated as "receive," to denote an immediacy in receiving as it conveys a sense of present action. This view interprets Jesus' words to mean "receive right now," and holds the day of the Lord's resurrection as marking the transition from the terms of the old covenant to those of the new covenant. The old creation began with the breath of God; the new creation began with the breath of God the Son.

Read Jeremiah 31:31–34; Hebrews 7:7–25; 1 Corinthians 2:10–16.

Questions:

What are the benefits of the new covenant?

_____

_____

How do you experience these benefits in your own life?

_____

_____

What is the reason God sent the Holy Spirit?

_____

_____

How does the Spirit's presence manifest in your own life?

_____

_____

Word Wealth—*Love*

Love: Greek *phileo* (fil-eh'-oh); Strong's #*5368*: To be fond of, care for affectionately, cherish, take pleasure in, have personal attachment for. This type of love is most often dependent upon feeling.

Love: Greek *agapao* (ag-ah-pah'-o); Strong's #*25*: Unconditional love, love by choice and by an act of the will. The word denotes unconquerable benevolence and undefeatable goodwill.

Behind the Scenes

Peter had denied Jesus three times. The Lord gave him a threefold opportunity to reaffirm his devotion. Jesus asked Peter twice if he bore *agape* love for Him. Peter responded with a claim of *phileo*. Peter wasn't prepared to make the commitment of *agape* love, so he offered all he thought he could give.

The third time, Jesus asked Peter if he loved Him with *phileo* love, inquiring if Peter even had the affection that he claimed. Peter could only appeal to the Lord's divine nature as proof of his sincerity.

Read 1 Corinthians 13; Romans 8:38–39; 1 Corinthians 2:9; Galatians 5:6; Ephesians 2:1–7; 1 John 4:7–21.

Questions:

Have you ever applied the definition of love in 1 Corinthians 13 to the love God has toward you?

✎ _____

_____

How could recognition of God's offer of this kind of love change the way in which you relate to Him?

✎ _____

_____

How do you understand the phrase "faith working through love" (Galatians 5:6)?

✎ _____

_____

How should this affect your walk of faith?

✎ _____

_____

What type of love do you offer the Lord?

✎ _____

_____

Record Your Thoughts

Questions:

What new revelations or renewed convictions have you experienced in this session?

✎ _____

_____

How will this impact your life and/or ministry?

✎ _____

_____

What steps do you intend to take to show forth the glory of God in a greater degree in your life?

✎ _____

_____

_____

Conclusion

To the New Testament disciple, godly living is living in, through, and for Jesus. Godliness includes three elements: love, obedience, and unity. By living godly lives, we learn to see things as God does and adopt His Word as our only standard.

To experience a life beyond the ordinary, you must exalt Jesus in your life and service, recognizing that love for your Lord results in obeying Him and laying down your life for others. Out of love for Him, you must commit yourself to the unity of the church and practice Christian citizenship as revealed through Jesus' life and ministry.

The sessions of this guide were designed to lead you into an abundant life, a life filled with meaning, purpose, and eternal value. It is a how-to guide to experiencing life far beyond what this world has to offer.

Let's review the Kingdom Keys of the twelve sessions of this study. Consider how each affects your life and ministry and how each can lead you to abundant life.

1. **Jesus Before All**

✎ _____

_____

2. **We Are Formed for a Purpose**

✎ _____

_____

3. We Have a Glorious Hope

_____

_____

4. He Quenches Our Thirst

_____

_____

5. We Are in His Image

_____

_____

6. Called Outside Our Comfort Zone

_____

_____

7. Depend on the Author

_____

_____

8. Desire Truth

_____

_____

9. Know the Mind of Christ

_____

_____

10. We Are Empowered to Serve

_____

_____

11. Receive the Helper

_____

_____

12. **Glorify God in All Things**

✎_____

_____

If you desire life beyond the meager offerings of this world, take to heart the words of John, the disciple whom Jesus loved. In this gospel you will find all you need to lead you into a life that far exceeds anything you could ask or imagine. John knew how to live beyond the ordinary. Through his words you, too, can find extraordinary life!

Ephesians 3:14–21

> For this reason I bow my knees to the Father of our Lord Jesus Christ, from whom the whole family in heaven and earth is named, that He would grant you, according to the riches of His glory, to be strengthened with might through His Spirit in the inner man, that Christ may dwell in your hearts through faith; that you, being rooted and grounded in love, may be able to comprehend with all the saints what is the width and length and depth and height—to know the love of Christ which passes knowledge; that you may be filled with all the fullness of God. Now to Him who is able to do exceedingly abundantly above all that we ask or think, according to the power that works in us, to Him be glory in the church by Christ Jesus to all generations, forever and ever. Amen.

Faith Alive

No matter what else is said about the gospel story, the bedrock is that the story is true. Jesus came into human history; ministered in a flesh-and-blood body to real people; and suffered, died, was buried, and rose again from the grave, conquering death forever. It all happened. We have eyewitness accounts affirming the veracity of these events and many more that haven't even been recorded. Jesus is not a fantasy, a wish-fulfillment, a legend concocted by people who desperately wanted to believe in someone who could guarantee their immortality. We have the best evidence in the world that all this is absolutely true. Our faith really is founded on fact. We don't have to leap into the abyss of incredulity.

By supplying us with such strong historical documents that archaeologists and Bible scholars have verified time and time again, God is telling us that He has no problems with our checking things out. He welcomes it. He has nothing to hide and so much to give.

But all the facts in the world won't save anyone until they put their trust in the One to whom history testifies. If you haven't already, come and put your trust in Him—either to receive everlasting life or to walk more closely with Him. It doesn't matter. He welcomes all who come to Him by faith exclaiming as Thomas did, "My Lord and my God!" (John 20:28).

And as He may have already been received by you as your Savior and Lord—go forward, praising Him for power to live for His glory, beyond the ordinary!

ADDITIONAL OBSERVATIONS